Whatever, Mom

Hip Mama's
Guide to Raising a Teenager

Ariel Gore
with Maia Swift

Seal Press

**WHATEVER, MOM: HIP MAMA'S GUIDE TO
RAISING A TEENAGER**

© 2004 by Ariel Gore

Published by
Seal Press
An Imprint of Avalon Publishing Group Incorporated
1400 65th Street, Suite 250
Emeryville, CA 94608

ISBN 1-58005-089-1

9 8 7 6 5 4 3 2 1

Designed by PDBD
Printed in the United States of America by Malloy
Distributed by Publishers Group West

Some names and identifying characteristics of individuals mentioned
have been changed to protect their privacy.

The disordered family
is full of dutiful children and parents.
The disordered society
is full of loyal patriots.

—Lao-tzu, *Tao Te Ching*

Contents

Things That Keep Us Up at Night   133

Waiting Up • Who's on Drugs? • Do Not Feel Like a Freak •
Brood • I Completely Shut Down • Is Talking Overrated? • "I Am
an Original" • The Color of Growing Up • That Has Made Me
Stronger • Lock Them In or Lock Them Out? • Fat and Imaginary
Fat • Suicide • Uncle Sam Is a Pusher • Why Do I Bother? •
Things That Keep *Me* Up at Night, by Maia Swift

Time Moving Forward   199

My Daughter Doesn't Think I Am a Shithead Anymore • Five-
Foot-Four • What's Enough • I Wouldn't Wish for Any Other •
For All We Know • Go Ask Inga • In Twenty Years, by Maia
Swift • Adults Will Try to Show You That It Doesn't Exist •
Spirit • What Religion Do I Belong To? • *Buona Sera, Bella
Mamma* • Comfort Food • Go, Teen, Go!

Whatever, Mom

The Way I Dreamed It

Here's the way I dreamed it: My daughter and I would glide into her teen years, our tight bond intact. With the steady stream of grown-up eccentrics wandering in and out of our lives, she'd have no reason to rebel. She'd ease into whatever identity she wanted to project—punk or goth, hippie or politico. My own musical tastes would keep up with the times, and together we'd rock out to the top forty on the alternative charts. Since I am a sex-positive and easygoing mama, my daughter would freely ask me about anything she had on her mind. I'd tell her the truth, and she'd follow my advice, because even though we'd get along like comrades, we *wouldn't* be best friends: We'd be mother and daughter—I wisely pointing her in the right direction, she proudly on her way. Lovely and boring.

And why shouldn't I have imagined it that way? When my kid was in elementary school, she was a smaller, cooler version of me. Sure, life changed and moved forward with each passing year . . . a new privilege here, a childhood toy tossed aside there. Nothing drastic. My daughter was slowly moving toward self-sufficiency. By age eleven she could get herself to school and back. She could fix a simple meal and put together a complex outfit. She could design a dream home and recognize a Georgia O'Keeffe painting. With some prompting, she could remember to wear a coat when it was cold, remember her homework assignments, and remember what time she had to be at tae kwon do.

I taught her my politics, my values, my fashion sense. And she was making those things her own. We went to protests together. We traveled the world. We thought the same things were beautiful, the same things scary. I was a zinester, she was a zinester. I was a writer, she was an artist. I wore black, she wore black. She was, essentially, Mini-Me—custom raised for my lifestyle.

And then one day she woke up, put on a pink shirt, and announced her plan to try out for the cheerleading team.

My eyes widened. I took a deep breath.

She said, "Mom, I know you might not support my decision."

"That's right," I nodded, then exhaled. "But I support *you.*"

She bit her lip. "I'll raise all the money for my uniform."

"Yes, you will. And I'll be there at all the games."

She'd warned me, when she was twelve: *"Having a baby or a kid might be hard, but you get to raise it in your world. When you're raising a teenager, you have to go into their world."* Into her world. But how?

Sometimes in a crowd, when I see her out of the corner of my eye, or from afar, I don't even recognize her. In my mind's eye, I just register a teenager or young woman—fifteen or twenty-two. She's got long brown hair with blonde streaks in it. She wears a fuzzy white sweater, a heart on a chain around her neck, black boot-cut jeans, Adidas. She's about my height—on the short side for a grownup, but too tall to be a kid. She's slender, composed, blasé. She's cool in a princessy sort of way. The kind of girl who probably wouldn't have spoken to me when I was that age.

I'm nearsighted. And anyway, she doesn't make eye contact until she has to. Embarrassed to see me. Embarrassed to be seen with me. But she comes closer. I do a double take. When I realize who she is, she suddenly appears smaller. Younger. She becomes a child—ten or twelve.

I refocus. This girl-woman is my baby. I see her infant-smooth skin under the pale face powder. Yet here she stands, thirteen years old, strong, vulnerable.

When I pick her up from school, I sometimes forget to wear my shoes. When she fails to look both ways before crossing the street, I scold her like she's five. I correct her friends when they say that Mexicans speak "Mexican." I tell her boyfriends they have to come in through the front door instead of using the back window. I shout at neighborhood kids not to threaten each other with big sticks.

She wants me to stop it. *Into her world.* But I hardly recognize her there.

At home, when no one is looking, she comes back into my world— if only for a few minutes or hours. She wants to talk about the way things were when *I* was a kid. Or when she was a baby. She wants me to brush her hair. She wants me to tuck her in. She wants me to lie with her as she falls asleep.

"Mama? Don't leave me."

I lie down, cuddle up next to her.

"Mama? I can't get to sleep."

I tell her to think about the Sierras, about a lake she knows well, to close her eyes and picture the whole scene.

"Mama?" she sits up a little. "The kids at school are smoking dope."

"Huh?"

"How old do you think kids should be before they smoke dope?"

It takes me a minute to readjust to the turn the conversation has taken, to the turns the years have taken. I clear my throat. "They probably shouldn't smoke it at all. But if they have to smoke it, they should wait until high school. I mean, no offense to your age group, but most of your friends can't get to Noah's and back with a half-dozen garlic bagels without getting distracted. You don't have that many brain cells to spare."

She laughs. "You have to say that because you're the *mom.*"

"True enough," I admit. "I'm biased. But I'll talk to you about anything you want to talk about. If you ever feel uncomfortable asking me things, Moe and Krystee and Inga are other good people to talk to, OK?"

"OK," she yawns.

She looks so little. Sleepy-eyed. Needy.

In the morning she'll apply a thick layer of face powder and ask me to drop her off a block away from school so as not to be seen with me.

Into her world.

Here's a card Maia wrote for a friend's thirteenth birthday:

Sup Sammi Girl!

It's the big 1-3! Know what that means? You're a teen! Now's your opportunity to: Get wild/crazy and blame it on your hormones, sneak out with all your girls in your parents' brand new BMW and still blend in, and last but not least, have a chance to be tak'n seriously (just playin'!!), and even though it's

just the beginning of your "teenhood," it's only seven years. So,
you bring the map, I'll bring the shot glasses and let's paaaty!!
(I'm just joking, Mr. & Mrs. Jackson!)

Lotsa Luv,
Maia

The big 1-3.

Poor Mr. and Mrs. Jackson.

Poor me!

Our kids' teen years constitute the most-feared period of a parent's life. From the time they're babies, we're warned about the horrors to come. "Just you wait," we're told. As if our new-parent culture shock and suddenly sleepless nights are nothing compared to What Will Come.

We dread adolescence. We deny it will happen to *our* family. *I'll be a different kind of parent,* we tell ourselves. We won't give our teens anything to rebel against. The worlds we've raised them in—our worlds—are beautiful, exciting, diverse. Our children won't *need* to break away.

We fear adolescence for a lot of reasons. We worry about our kids' safety. We don't want to lose control. We don't want our kids to experience pain—and we remember so much pain from those years in our own lives. It's only human that as parents, we want to be loved and accepted. We don't want our every comment picked apart and found lacking, thrown back in our faces. We don't want to go to football games or enter worlds outside our comfort zones. And, frankly, we don't want to get old. If our children are young adults, what does that make *us?* Our culture teaches us to be scared of teenagers, but also to glorify the teen years. The adolescent appearance is considered the height of beauty and sex appeal. Teen culture—when it's not depicted as depraved and self-destructive—is seen as incomparably cool, revolutionary, *fun.* John Cougar Mellencamp told us it would be downhill as soon as we let go of age sixteen. And so we hung on. We believed him. If our kids are now approaching Jack and Diane's age, how *totally* long gone are all the thrills of our own lives?

We're warned that the parent-teen relationship, for its part, is intrinsically adversarial. Our kids will be raging wild against us and hating everything about us down to the way we brush our teeth. They'll be making life choices so far from anything we ever would have chosen for them that we'll be hating *them,* too. Defiant monsters.

It's true that our kids will not be us. But the real and lived separation of our worlds, it turns out, is far from anything that old songs or conventional wisdom ever taught us. Teenage kids are complex, fragile, feisty. The life phase they're going through is full of optimism, curiosity, tribulation, and unexpected twists. Becoming the parent of a teenager is just as myth-shattering, mind-blowing, heartbreaking, and awesome as becoming a parent in the first place. But it doesn't have to be the end of all that was good and loving about our families.

It's also true that we're not sixteen anymore. But John Cougar Mellencamp was full of it. For most of us, hanging on to sixteen would be hanging on to our pre-experienced, pre-initiated, pre-intuitive selves. The road to maturity is a rough one. We don't want to admit that we've been through it. Our scars show. And judging from the wealth of the makers of Botox, antiwrinkle cream, and hair dye, most of us are less than proud of our scars. Still, I dare you to find one grownup who honestly wants to go back to being who they were then. We mourn our youthful appearance, but we cherish our inner development. We want to be sixteen again, but not without knowing what we know now. We want our kids to be sixteen, too—aren't they beautiful?—but we want them to carry *our* grown-up wisdom and values into *their* world. This cannot be. Our kids will carry some of our wisdom—that's what evolution's all about—but only some of it. They'll trash some of our values, too—that's also what evolution is about.

Adolescence includes some serious lows, but many of those lows are necessary rites of passage. Our kids are beginning to take control of their own destinies, and they're going to have to do it in their own ways.

As parents, then, how do we deal? What are our responsibilities at this point? I figure our tasks are eightfold: to be ourselves; to pay attention; to speak our truths and do our best to communicate whatever wisdom we have; to cultivate compassion about the fact that these years can be extremely difficult for both ourselves and our kids; to be fierce about the things that truly matter to us; to lighten up and let go of the things that are trivial; to accept that all we can do sometimes is pray for the best outcome; and, yes, to let go of sixteen ourselves.

The way I dreamed it, time was standing still. This book is an attempt to chronicle time moving forward.

The fact that this forward motion causes me to occasionally burst into tears without warning—when I see a littler kid hiking with his parents or when I realize I can finally afford that wooden playhouse my daughter no longer wants—suggests to me that the trip is worthwhile. Tears are rivers that take us someplace. Through the stereotypes and fears. Through the grief and the magic. Into adolescence. But this time, as a parent. As a mother. Into her world. And back to my own.

Lovely, and never boring.

In/Dependence

*It is so hard for us to let our children into the vulnerable
spaces of our lives because we don't want them to know
how raw Real Life can be. My God, how we wish that
we could make the world perfect for them. How we wish
we could offer them miraculous wisdoms that would
carry them from mountain-top experience to mountain-
top experience without any slips, or falls, or failures. We
want for them the life we envisioned for ourselves.*

—Esther Davis-Thompson, mother of ten,
Raising Up Queens

First Things First

At the risk of sounding a wee bit academic, I want to make one thing clear: Adolescence is a social construction. I turn from you now for emphasis, chalk in hand, reach for the blackboard on the far facing wall, and write:

Adolescence

Is

a

Social

Construction.

Tell a Third-World mama that her kids need a few years to "find themselves" before they start working and she's likely to laugh in your face. Among Western families, adolescence as we know it has only been around for a few generations. *Teenager.* Before the 1920s, the word wasn't even in the dictionary.

If you're not sure how your great-great-grandmother spent her teen years, find out. If you can't find out, here's a likely scenario: She started working at twelve; married at fourteen; was widowed at nineteen; and raised up your great-grandma with love, hard work, and fierceness.

Even your most aristocratic ancestors never knew these long seasons of middle school and orthodontia, Ritalin and yo-yo diets, standardized tests and summer vacations, call waiting and CD Walkmans, football practice and study-abroad programs, learner's permits and college choices.

Sure, some things about adolescence are universal and timeless. Take puberty. One minute our kids are sitting around minding their own business, and the next—cometlike—their bodies and minds and hormones and hearts go rampantly wild. In a creeping instant, sweet-suffering, black-and-white childhood transforms itself into awesome, overwhelming, Technicolor teenagehood. It happens to virtually everyone—African, European, Asian, First Nation, rich, poor, middle-class—and has throughout the ages. There is a flush magnificence, a burst of creativity. There is the energy and anticipation and confusion of discovering the world anew and for the first time. There is sexual development and all kinds of abstract thinking. There is blow-me-away crazy beautiful traumatic first romantic love. For virtually everyone. But the near-decade we give our kids to swim through it all—years set aside for individuation and rebellion, development and self-expression, angst and trying-on of identities—these years constitute an invented stage, a big fat social construction, a *luxury*.

I'm not saying that the next time your kid refuses to do the dishes, stomps into his room, and starts blaring the latest hip-hop album through the house, you ought to barge in, smash his stereo, and scream in his face, "How'd you like to be working in a sweatshop, mister?!" I'm just saying that it's a whole lot of nurture and only a smattering of nature that has our families acting so crazy for so long. And yes, it's a great *luxury* that has you banging your head against the wall right about now.

The adolescent years are an amazing privilege, but that doesn't make them easy, fair, or fun. Our kids are preparing to go out into the world without us, and we're learning to let go. There is a flush magnificence—but there is also a bombardment of media images, a bewildering sense of freedom, and a nasty little cultural blueprint for self-destruction. Our daughters get their periods, they grow breasts and hips, and the world tells them they are fat, tells them to shut up, tells them to paint their faces, tells them to mold themselves into prey. Our sons grow into their full height, their voices deepen, and the world tells them they aren't cute anymore, tells them they shouldn't be hanging on their mamas anymore, tells them to stop crying and reach for the available arsenal, tells them to mold themselves into predators.

I can hear my great-great-grandmother now: She's weeping in her ocean grave. Is this what she worked so hard for? This long-suffering luxury of a transition into adulthood and the inevitable day when her children's children's children's children's children would stand in the kitchen, cross their arms, lock eyes with their mothers for an instant, then refocus somewhere near the ceiling, let out an exaggerated sigh, and say, "God, Mom. You are *such* a *dork.*"

I guess if I were a better person, I would have met this day in my own family with confidence and understanding. I'd have seen the event in its full historical and cultural context. And then maybe I wouldn't have had to bite my tongue to keep from shouting, "I gave you my youth, kid. And *this* is the thanks I get?" But I am not a better person. And, let's face it, having a little kid who looked up to me like I was the

Queen of Cool was a real ego boost for me. And having a teenager in the house is something like coming down hard off ecstasy. My teeth hurt. My back hurts. And I'm not sure if my eardrums or my self-esteem can handle seven years of this shit. And yes, I know, *intellectually,* that a woman should never do anything she wants to hear "thank you" for, but knowing a thing intellectually is different from really *knowing* it, and this is where I find myself, and this *is* the thanks I get:

The Eight Most Embarrassing Things about My Mother

Maia Swift

1. Dyes her hair every time she gets a gray—and it's obvious
2. Wears her own company's T-shirts with ripped jeans and biker boots as if she's some kind of punk revolutionary
3. Acts like a little kid around me and my friends, like when she walks in and says, "Are we having a slumber party, girls?!?" (I know it's a joke, but we're not laughing *with* you, Mom.)
4. Wears outfits that show half her cleavage and midriff
5. Wears outfits that show her '90s tattoos
6. Argues with me when we're shopping and wants me to get jeans two sizes too big for me so they'll last through the school year when both me and the teenage saleswoman know the jeans won't be in style by the end of the school year
7. Even after I ask her if she can drop me off a block away from my destination, insists on driving me the whole way
8. Waits for me outside of school and then, if I'm late, actually *gets out of the car*

◎   ◎   ◎

I mean, all right. Fair enough. I'm no stranger to the *total* humiliation of having a dorky mother. (Although I think the word of choice was "lame" when I was thirteen—as in, "God, Mom. You are *so lame.*") And, all right, I'll admit that I do, on occasion, take some perverse pleasure in acting *exceptionally* dorky around her friends for no other reason than to mess with her and her budding sense of normalcy and independence. And, all right, I'll acknowledge that I failed to lead a successful revolution razing all these social constructions to the ground before she was born. And here we are, living right now in America. So let's do it. Adolescence. *Where shall we begin?*

Good Morning

On a good morning, I'm the first one up.

In the damp, violet Portland dawn, coffee tastes like hope. Maybe there'll be a little sunshine today. I answer a few e-mails; delete the ads for penile enlargement, housewife porn, and low mortgage rates. I fantasize that someday the inbox will be empty, dealt with.

Drinking coffee on my back porch, I watch over the fence as my down-the-street neighbor leaves for work in the first light of day. My yard smells like clover. I can hear the bearded survivalist I saw passed out on the sidewalk last night rattling bottles from my recycling bin now.

Back in my kitchen office, I glance over the calendar entries and remember where I'm supposed to be today, what I'm supposed to be doing. There's nothing out of the ordinary in terms of responsibilities. Just the standard writing and teaching, shuttling Maia to and from her various activities.

I open my diary and jot down a few lines; open the book project I'm working on, jot down a few chapter notes; and expand on yesterday's missives.

An hour alone and then my partner mumbles her way out of bed, makes more coffee. She switches on the TV, and all at once the tragedies of the world are paraded through our living room. *Good Morning America*. Diane Sawyer wears an awkward blue turtleneck, but she's smiling. Good morning.

The mother of a murdered woman is giving a live press conference on the West Coast. Tears stream down her pale face as she reads her prepared statement. "My only daughter . . . my best friend . . ." Her cries break into wails. Her grief is fresh, hot. And I grieve with her. She is speaking to me of her loss, but soon my mind wanders. I am looking at her on the screen through sleepy eyes—contacts still not in—and I see myself. *Would I give a press conference if my daughter was murdered? What would I say? Would I feel like a failure for being unable to protect her? Would I wish I'd had more children? Would I cry like that, publicly?*

And so I'm sitting on the couch. I'm crying for the woman on TV, crying for myself, for my daughter. This is real. A mother can take care of a child for ten years, twenty years, thirty years. And then some smirking, suave husband can whisk her away, slit her throat, dump her body in the bay. Cut back to Diane Sawyer. She looks serious for an instant, then smiles again, moves on to news of war, stock markets, and the latest pop single. And I'm still crying for my daughter, who is very much alive, breathing deeply, sleeping in her soft, warm bed. Maybe I'm practicing for worst-case scenarios—as if imagining hell can soothe my fear of it, take its power away.

"Maia? Are you up?"

"No," she grumbles.

I enter the blue mayhem of her room. The carpet is barely visible under the clothes and shoes and CDs and pompoms and teen magazines and pictures of friends. The walls are covered with tae kwon do certificates, cheerleading awards, more pictures of friends, makeup ads, posters of kittens, and hip-hop stars. 2Pac looks so young to me now.

"Maia—it's past eight o'clock."

I try dragging her out of bed; she's almost as big as I am. She goes limp. She's practicing for a sit-in. She's tired. She's messing with me.

"Come on, honey . . ." I play along, appreciative that we're both alive. I slip my arms under her knees and back, attempt to lift her. I'm nostalgic for the days when I could scoop her up easily, slip clothes onto her sleeping body, bundle her into the car. She has to ready herself now. She protests for as long as she can, finally surrenders to the reality of the morning.

Jeans are dug out of the pile on the floor and "Have you seen my white sweat jacket?" Powdery pastel makeup on and "Where's my brush?" Hair straightened and re-curled with hot medieval-looking irons and gloopy creams. The chaos of homework stuffed into the backpack that's ripped and stained and scrawled-on with a black Sharpie: "I'm too sexy for my pack." I guess she is. She wants a new one. But I'm trying to stall her until summertime. Until fall.

"Where's that note you were supposed to sign?" she wants to know. And "Can I have two dollars?" And "Oh, actually, can you make that five?" And "Oh my god, I forgot about the *science* homework." And "No, I am *not* gonna be late! *God, Mom.*" All aflutter and monkey stress. School starts at nine A.M., a relatively civilized hour. I'm dreading the year it goes back to eight.

So it's four minutes to nine now and we're finally in the car. Then, "Oh! Wait! Can I go back inside and get *one* thing?"

I say "sure" before realizing that the forgotten item is a tube of

Tootsie Roll–flavored lip gloss. I mean, *holy crap*. I am sitting in the middle of the street with the car running for a tube of Tootsie Roll–flavored lip gloss. This cannot be real. But it is. Suddenly my New Age California upbringing kicks in: *Be here now. In the middle of the street with car running, waiting for Tootsie Roll–flavored lip gloss. Breathe in, breathe out. Accept it.*

She leaps into the passenger seat and we're off, weaving through rushed morning traffic, around beeping school buses and erratic SUV drivers. We negotiate the skateboarding boys a block away from campus, barely avoid a tragic collision with a hackey-sack punk girl who has suddenly hurled herself into the middle of the street. I screech to a halt, save her life. And she slams her pale hand onto the hood of my car and snarls, "Fuck you!"

We are alive. Appreciate it.

"Just pull up a few yards closer," Maia is telling me. She wants to avoid the hackey-sack girl, who's dressed in full '80s zippered mall-punk black polyester, but she doesn't want me to get close enough to the hip-hop and "prep" crowds to humiliate her. "Right here. Right here. *Stop!*"

I inch forward a little more just to torment her. "Have a good day, honey. I love you."

She smiles without looking back, "You too." And she climbs out of the car and into another good morning at middle school.

A Chocolate-Coated Sour Tart

I asked fifteen- and sixteen-year-olds, "What does middle school taste like?"

> Winterfresh chewing gum
> Cup O' Noodles
> Watermelon lip gloss
> Cafeteria food
> Toxic drinking-fountain water
> Bitter
> Really nasty
> Sour
> A chocolate-coated sour tart
> Sour pears
> Sweet and sour
> Blue cotton candy
> An overripe grape
> Adidas shoes

A bad movie
Elmer's Glue
Pepperoni pizza
Microwave popcorn
Marshmallows
Dissected squid
The worm in the apple
The beets your parents
    make you eat
Dirt
Mud
Play-Doh
Old blue bubble gum
Like crap
I'm not sure. I never took a bite. One
    day I licked the hallway wall. Does
    that count? I got a few chips of
    paint.

Individuation

Accept them. *Realize that your children are individuals with their own personalities, likes and dislikes. Don't try to force them to live the life that's ideal to you. Instead, respect their unique talents and what's important to them. Don't freak out over their changing bodies—they are still very much kids, and they still need your love and approval, even if they don't show it.*

—Cary, 16

All of a sudden their moods became mercurial, language became peppered with expletives, and they knew everything about everything, while I knew nothing. I found myself being challenged and engaged in lots of power struggles. Raised voices. Digging-in of heels. Questioning from them whenever limits were set.

—Mama Maureen

Individuation. What is it? It's the process of becoming oneself. Separate. It starts at birth—the first big separation from mama. It surfaces as a major issue in toddlerhood (do "No! No! No!" and "It is *mine!*" ring any bells?). Kids spend the next ten years becoming more and more autonomous. And then puberty. It occurs like a revelation: *I do not have to be like my mother.* Or more intensely: *I have nothing in common with anyone in my family. That I ended up with them was a cosmic mistake.*

Their brains are kicking into grown-up gear, and they're asking, *What does it mean to be fundamentally alone in the world?* Here come philosophical thinking, hypothetical reasoning, and new decision-making skills. I don't know—we gave them these brains, and all of a sudden they want to use them. They're on the road to independence and self-government.

I remember my own mom's lament when I was thirteen and my sister sixteen. She sat at the dining-room table with another mother friend and, only half joking, bemoaned her fate: "I always taught my kids to question authority. I didn't mean for them to question *my* authority."

If you're like me, mama hawk, maybe you didn't let your kids traipse around the neighborhood much when they were little, but what can you say now? No? You can't be out of my sight until you're twenty-one? So off they go without any adult supervision, and now they have to decide for themselves: *Do I give the beggar on the corner a dime or do I just walk on by? Do I use my lunch money to buy a sandwich like I promised, or do I buy seven candy bars and lie about it?* If they run over the neighbor's cat with their scooter, do they tell someone or do they dash home and hide? And when the creepy dude who doesn't look so creepy invites them inside to play a game of Nintendo, do they follow him? Decisions. Trivial and serious. Decisions about safety, ethics, and self-nourishment. If they're lucky, they've learned a thing or two from the thoughtful grownups who've been in their lives up until now, and they've got a good sense of intuition. If they're lucky, they won't have to get hurt too badly as they develop that intuition into the guardian angel it can be. In any case, our kids do the best they can with the information they have. And when they need help they often ask . . . *a friend.*

The separation happens in fits and starts. But our kids are becoming less and less emotionally dependent on us. We're big dorks. Or we're clueless. We're old-fashioned. Or we're only telling the half-truths parents have to tell because we don't want them to take risks. We don't understand how things are done *now.* Or we don't understand *them.* So they start focusing on relationships outside the family. Suddenly neighbor Suzie's opinion of that new pair of jeans at Forever 21 outweighs what mama thinks by about one hundred to one. Gone are the days when I could buy my girl-child an outfit without checking in with the fashion police. If you want to shop for your teen, you'd better hope you're the same size, because guess who's gonna get stuck with all the reject clothes? Yep. I'm spending the winter in a baby-blue Performance-fleece hoodie I was convinced Maia would just *love.*

"Look what I got you at Buffalo Exchange, honey!"

Blank stare. The now-familiar eye roll not unlike the look I get when I suggest she do the dishes. She sighs. "God, Mom."

The good news (besides that I don't really mind baby-blue Performance fleece) is that a grumpy child at home doesn't necessarily equal a grumpy child in the world. If I want to know if my kid has any manners, I'd better not rely on observing the way she reacts to me. The season Maia was the surliest at home, she was voted "Most

Friendliest" at school. Who knew?

The season I worried that she was retreating too far into herself—becoming dangerously shy and withdrawn—her math teacher called to tell me that my social butterfly of a girl-woman was disrupting his classroom. And a week later, she was voted captain of her cheerleading team. My free child. I always told her she could be anything she wanted to be: punk, goth, hippie, politico. My free child became the captain of her cheerleading team.

And so there I am at the games, clapping politely next to the *insane* football parents who scream, "Knock somebody down, number fifty-four!" and then proceed to fight with *each other* over whatever illegal play I don't understand and god-knows-what yard line or kick. I mean, *honestly*. My mother thought the 1980s mosh pits were scary?

Anyway. Back to individuation. Our kids are becoming more and more themselves. Trying on various identities. Taking more responsibility for their own lives and their own decisions. Practicing for that day in the not-so-far-off future when they'll live and deal competently on their own, relying mostly on people other than us—their friends and chosen families. In the meantime, they'll probably keep us in the loop when it comes to long-term decisions—where they're thinking about going to college or whether they want to be auto mechanics or philosophers. But when it comes to short-term decisions like what to wear, which concert to save up for, and whether to go to the dance with goober #1 or goober #2, they're ready to go it alone, or with advice from their buddies.

When I asked my daughter how I could best help her through these complex times, she said, "Stop harassing me and stop abandoning me!"

"Those things seem contradictory, honey."

She shook her head, wouldn't explain any further.

"Do you mean that you feel like I'm abandoning you because I don't take care of you like I used to, and that the only attention you get from me is nagging—like 'Do your homework. Do these chores. Why are you dating that boy?'"

She nodded.

I understood. But I wasn't sure how to fix it.

When I asked my high school students to offer a little advice, they articulated the same paradox.

I think parents should treat their teenagers as adults. Parents need to respect our life decisions and realize we're not kids anymore! Give us a little more freedom, but still watch out for us and still care. Watch us closely but give us room. Give us a choice but let us decide. Know where we are and trust us. Give us hope and let us know you're counting on us. Make us feel loved but give us space. Be a parent, not a best friend.

—Rashelle, 15

Rule #1 is you have to give us some space because we go through a lot these days and sometimes we want to be left alone. Rule #2 is you have to care. Ask, How was your day? and How are you? An occasional I love you would be nice because sometimes we feel alone and scared. Rule #3 is give us rules to live by. Otherwise we will screw up our lives, and then what? After high school everyone will have left and we'll be like a mouse trying to find the cheese he knows he will never find.

—Corinne, 16

It's crazy-making contradictory. *Watch us closely! Give us space! We want to be left alone! We don't like feeling so alone!* But as we remember our own teen years, or talk more with our kids, we start to get it—intellectually, anyway. What I think they're saying is this: Back off when it comes to micromanaging our lives. Let us start managing our own lives. But don't withdraw your emotional support. Choose your battles, but do intervene when we're truly screwing up.

It's a tricky balance, but our kids are learning self-reliance. And self-reliance can't be taught in the way that counting or reading could be. It's a process of trial and error. And trial. And error.

While all of this is going on, our kids are also developing their own morals and values. Hopefully, the building blocks for their value systems fell into place when they were younger—building blocks like compassion and a sense of justice. But now they can think about right and wrong in more abstract ways. They can begin to analyze situations and make decisions based on principles, individual rights, interpersonal relationships, empathy, and kindness. Our kids' political thinking becomes more sophisticated, too, often tending toward the rigid in the early teen years and easing up as they gain more experience. Don't be surprised, then, if your twelve-year-old is a rabid pro-lifer who mellows out at fourteen when his first friends have abortions and ends up carrying a We Won't Go Back sign at a pro-choice rally when he's sixteen. Teenagers aren't schizophrenic. They're just dealing—the best they can—with a complex world.

[As a teenager myself] I was sometimes repelled, sometimes in need of my mother. Bearing this in mind, I tried to cool down a lot of moments between my daughter and me. At age thirteen, she wanted to be free to decide where to live. There was this really

29

nice boarding school near Hamburg where many of her
schoolmates from Ibiza went now, and also where her
grandmother lived. She had a steady boyfriend at an early age
(as I did). So she was allowed to move in with him at my
mother's house. I missed her terribly, and I'm sure that she
missed us also, but we visited each other a lot and also spent
holidays together.

—Mama Nina

So that's individuation: the process of becoming oneself—the years when our kids become Young Republicans, and it's either a phase or it isn't. They look us in the eye and tell us that our values are dead wrong. They'll come around. Or they won't. And if they don't? They're still their own people. And that's exactly who we wanted them to be: themselves. This is the era in which our kids learn that they do not have to be just like us. If our kids find out later that there were things we were right about, at least it won't be because we told them so. They'll have discovered their own truths in their own time. If our kids find out that our values will never fit their lives, we can agree to disagree, supporting them whether or not we support their choices. And maybe they'll change *our* views a little bit in the process. We'll come around. Or we won't. And at the end of the day, if we're lucky, we'll be able to say that we did our best not to abandon them too often, not to harass them too much, to make them feel cared for, to give them their space. Because they just want to be able to find the cheese themselves, you know?

Where Were the Parents?

When the phone is ringing, and the instant messenger is beeping, and the stereo is blaring the booty-jam station too loud, and one kid's in the kitchen whining, "I'm hungry," while the other one's in the hallway demanding you find and wash a softball uniform immediately, and the bathroom is a disaster area of coconut shaving cream and tropical fruit shampoo and you're fifteen minutes late to wherever you were going—you can't remember where now—and your lover is moaning about something so completely irrelevant that you can't even make out the words, and you just spilled coffee on your new white shirt, and the one kid's still in the kitchen whining about hunger but apparently helpless to boil water for the instant noodles she says she wants, and some commentator on the TV news is complaining, "Where were the parents?" when reporting on the latest juvenile crime, and your shoes have been stolen by one of the kids because they were obviously just too good for Mom, and there's a teacher on the phone now using that tone of voice that tells you it's about time to pour yourself a drink, and the dog needs to be walked, and the doorbell's ringing and even though there are three people closer to the door than you are no one answers it, and there's an electric company cutoff notice on your desk, and the laundry pile is obscuring the path to the back exit, and you suddenly remember that you volunteered to make a triple-recipe of lasagna for some team potluck and you have no earthly idea where the pans are, it's perfectly all right for you to turn off all the media, scream, "Get it yourself!" and run yourself a nice, warm bath. All these people can get along just fine without you for an hour. They just don't want to.

Listen!

I asked a group of teenagers, "If you could offer parents of teens one piece of advice, what would it be?"

Don't let your kids be afraid to talk to you. If you're constantly saying things like, If you ever do X you're going to be grounded for the rest of your life! your kids are going to be too afraid to come to you when they really need you. For instance, be firm in your stance on no drinking alcohol, but don't let your kid be afraid to call you if they've been drinking and can't drive. I'd much rather have my kid call me for help than to have her be afraid and drive home drunk, risking her and other people's lives.

—Sam, 17

Ease up on the interrogation. You don't need to know who's dating who, who got in a fight with who. Quite frankly, we're not going to want to tell you if you're the one who asks.

—Phoebe, 16

I think the one thing that could make the relationship between my mom and me better is if she could see me as a young woman who will not fall if given the chance to fly instead of a little girl that needs a soft landing under her at all times.

—Grace, 14

The thing I find most tragic about the relationship of parents and teens is their lack of communication. At some point between the ages of ten and thirteen, parents take a step back to allow their children freedom to grow. The problem is that some of them give their kids too much space. It is vital that parents stay involved with their kids; then teenagers won't feel that they can't talk to their parents. Both of my parents died before I was a teenager, so I was raised by my grandmother. She is a devout Southern Baptist, and some of my choices have hurt her deeply, but she listens to me without judgment even when she disagrees with me. And she has become so much more open-minded because of it!

—Jamie, 18

Trust your teens. If you don't trust them and make them justify every action with a "tell me the truth," you're pushing them to go somewhere else.

—Rama, 15

What an opportunity! I'm assuming this advice will be submitted anonymously? God knows if my parents only knew I was writing this, my life of freedom would come to a horrible, and, more specifically, grounded, end. However, I'm hoping this advice will be taken seriously, in which case I've just been given an excellent chance to manipulate . . . or should I say improve *my parents', well, parenting.*

#1 Pay your son/daughter a large sum of money weekly. It will be used for school supplies.

#2 You really don't want to hurt your child's feelings, do you? So, when you go out of town, don't *make someone go and check up on them. It will show you have confidence in them. Hell, why don't you go out of town right now? The independence will be good for them.*

—Anonymous, 16

Why Can't You Be Normal?

*"Moooooom, you are so embarrassing!" I was told in a
stern whisper, "When my friends come over here, don't
say anything."*

*I went from the cool, youngish mom to the mom
who inevitably would say the exact wrong thing in the
presence of screeching seventh graders.*

*And now, just as my eldest enters eighth grade, I
have gone through a spiritual initiation in Lucumi, a
Cuban derivation of African traditional religion, and
am swathed in white garb from head to toe for the next
year. Now I am totally embarrassing. . . . And my wack-
ass religion is embarrassing, too. Little does my
daughter know the pleading I have done to my spirits
during sleepless nights that have helped her.*

Oh, but right—she doesn't believe in that "stuff."

—Mama Inga

When my son hit about age eleven, he began lamenting how abnormal we were, compared with his peers' parents, and how, on the one hand, it was embarrassing, and on another, it just made him feel different and uncomfortable. He began to want to fit in with his peers. That was, apparently, impossible because we were so different. We ate the wrong foods (organic, no junk, vegetarian, whole grains, soymilk, the works), did not dress stylishly, and often shopped in second-hand stores. We were too liberal, too outspoken; we did not practice a religion; and, worst of all, I did not shave my legs or underarms. I joked that I guessed I didn't have to worry that he would get his face pierced or dye his hair purple or green because his goal was to fit in, not stand out.

—Mama Faye

My daughter is never angry at society—just me. The whole world is my fault. Right now I just feel like teenagers have the power to destroy their parents and I might be the first parent to actually run away from home.

—Mama China

"God, Mom, why can't you be normal?"

"And why can't you dress more like Juliette and Tracey?"

"Why is your tattoo so *big?*"

"You're in your thirties now. They must have a Gap for Seniors or something at the mall where you can get some normal clothes."

"Why can't you get the car washed?"

"God, Mom."

"Why don't you work?"

"What religion are we, anyway?"

"The other moms dress normal."

"The other moms have normal jobs."

"The other moms have husbands."

"The other moms are in their forties."

"The other moms . . . are not you."

I know it's a teenager's job to reject her parents. It's silly to expect a teenage kid to understand the sacrifices a person—especially a parent—may have made to be true to herself in this world. Still, it hurts. I take the critiques seriously even as I watch other mom friends getting taken to task for being *too* normal. Their spike-wearing baby-punk teens and preteens constantly ask, "Why are you so mainstream?" I take it seriously, and it starts to make me sad. And I think, *You know what? I am sorry: I am sorry for bringing you into a world where "normal" wears pleated pants, where "normal" is war-mongering, where "normal" is nationalistic, nuclear, homophobic, antifeminist. You are not these things, girl-woman, but "normal" is.*

And I think, *You know what? I am sorry: I am sorry that the world has treated you differently because your family rents instead of owns. And I am sorry that I raised you in a culture I knew would judge you because of my age. I'm sorry that I didn't get a chance, before you were born, to lead a successful revolution to turn "normal" on its head. In my postrevolutionary world, "normal" would include me and our family. In that utopia, you could still rebel—you with your hip-hop music that makes your sex-positive parent and grandparents blush. You could still shock with your cheerleading accomplishments and your business-minded aspirations. You could still wow with your mosaic self-portraits set against starry skies.*

When our kids are in their early teens, they start seeing us as major freaks. They become aware of—and often internalize—whatever social stigmas we're up against. The kids of gays and lesbians, hairy-armpit hippies, religious folks, nonreligious folks, older parents, younger parents, immigrants, poor people, environmentalists, punks, artists, musicians, and alterna-whatevers suddenly have to contend with a world that thinks their families are unacceptable. The conservative bent of a lot of teenage kids is most pronounced for those in public schools, but virtually all of them go through a shift—from identifying with their own family's values to identifying with the larger culture's values. It will almost certainly pass, but for now it's part of the reality of having kids.

I want to accept this. I want to give my girl-woman full right to reject me and my wardrobe, to reject me and my musical tastes, to reject me and my penchant for Japanese pulp fiction. I want to give her full right to question my spiritual beliefs, my political leanings, my parenting limits. *But I cannot apologize for who I am.* I apologized as a kid. Too quiet. I apologized as a teenager. Too nomadic. I apologized as a new mom. Too poor. Too single. But I don't want to apologize anymore. Because I don't like right angles. And I'm not sorry.

No, I think, *I'm not sorry. This is who I am, whole and unmedicated. Me who works too hard, but never has a "real job." Me who dresses in Levi's and striped arm warmers. Me who makes mistakes. Still too quiet. Nomadic mind. Girl-woman, I give you me: human mother. It's all I have, but also all you need from me.*

There was a time when I was my daughter's everything—sole creator, sole nurturer, sole role model. She strained her neck looking up at me. Now that we're eye to eye, she sees through me. I am learning, slowly, to accept the demotion to all I ever was: human mother.

I sit back into my big purple couch, pop a beer. Impure thoughts start running through my mind, like, *How embarrassing can I possibly be?* The fantasies flip through my mind like a glorious slide show of possibilities: I'm at the mall wearing a big, pink sandwich board that says Maia Swift's Mother.

I'm in the bleachers at the next football game: I've got a purple mohawk and I'm screaming antiwar slogans at the evil fans.

That's me, clucking like a chicken through the halls of her middle school.

And, yes! There I am again—picking her up from tae kwon do wearing nothing but a Japanese bra that plays electronica Mozart.

"God, Mom. Why do you have such a weird look on your face?"

I smile, and say nothing.

Do Parents *Try* to Embarrass You?

Maia Swift

Being embarrassed about your parents, that's something everyone has to go through. When someone has a kid, something happens to them. They just don't understand things the same way anymore. Sometimes if you're lucky, they will remember when they were a kid, and they will wanna relate to you. I mean, that's cool, but it can get weird, especially if you're with your friends when it happens.

Parents have several ways of embarrassing you. I think my mom gets that she embarrasses me, but she thinks of it as some big joke. When I was little, my mom was the coolest mom on the block. I liked to show her off. All of my friends' moms were forty-five, and I had this mid-twenties mom, dying her hair and shopping at all the stores I shopped at. Now my mom is in her mid-thirties, has seven tattoos (one covered up), still dyes her hair multicolors, and listens to '80s women singers having their spiritual breakthroughs.

She's told me what my grandma used to do to embarrass her,

but it's not the same.

Sometimes they are *trying* to embarrass you, maybe to get back at you, or maybe to show they're really your parents. And sometimes they do it on accident. Maybe they're trying to relate to you, as if you were eight, and it didn't bother you, or maybe trying to mix their generation with ours. Trying to be cool, and having it blow up in their face.

I've been embarrassed by my mom a lot, in every possible way. *Wow,* wait, not *every* possible way, but any way is horrible.

The first time I was embarrassed by my mom that I can remember, was when I was in first or second grade. I was really young and I was trying to act older than my age and my mom was acting younger than a mom should. It was embarrassing because she was acting normal, not that anyone knew *that,* but when your mom is acting more your age then you, that's weird! That way people notice *you* more. Or if your friends are with you, and from that point on they think your mom is completely immature.

Now that I'm older, my mom isn't supposed to be my friend, not that I don't want her to be, but it's different from when I used to tell her everything, and wanted advice. Now I want a loose, yet very motherly mom. Like giving me a curfew, but also not asking me exactly when I'll be back, and making sure I'm not alone with a boy. My family and my social life are incredibly different, and shouldn't be mixed at all, or even meet for the slightest time.

When my mom hangs out, well not really "hangs out," but me and my friends are with her in the car going to the movies or something, sometimes she acts like she's having trouble with the road, as if she is lost, and all her attention is on the street signs, but like she's still listening. Another way she acts around my friends and me is by pretending to not be there. Actually, this makes me act even weirder, and I think, "What if she's actually paying attention, and listening to what we're saying, and thousands of questions are going through her head," like when you're walking down the street, and thousands of things go through your mind about what's going on around you. Except I'm getting annoyed with what I think is going through her mind. If that makes any sense, that's good, 'cause I don't really have any other way of putting it. I guess that what I think is going through her mind worries me, and I sit there in the car trying to tell myself that's not what she's thinking. When I'm with my mom and my group I start to act more like my mom. And at the time I do realize it, so I try to just nod my head and smile without saying cuss words, or anything else my mom spent her whole life telling me not to do, but doing herself.

There isn't really anything you can do about your mom or dad embarrassing you. You could try telling them to stop, lay it out for them and tell them just how you feel. But if someone had a really embarrassing parent and found out a way to cut it down a notch, then the world would stretch, and the problem would be less for all of us. I think it's something that can never be *properly* fixed, *or* you're super lucky to have such a flexible parent/parents.

Now, when my mom does something embarrassing, I smile a sweet, sarcastic smile, open my eyes *really* big, and say, "Mom, *stop!*"—and then I laugh a sarcastic laugh. That gets her to stop, but not permanently (of course).

Being Me

Maybe it's a silly question, but I asked fifteen- and sixteen-year-olds, "What is embarrassing?"

> My parents
> Looking like a fool
> Losing control
> Being human
> Adolescence
> Pretending you know stuff you don't
> Feeling dumb
> A burning face and sweaty palms
> Driving a ghetto car
> Failing a test
> Deception
> Throwing up on Grandma
> Being fat
> Losing

My sister
Being me
Staring at a girl without realizing it
Farting
My dad
Being late to class
Publication
This question

Mad Sick

> *Because they challenge us to the limits of our open-*
> *mindedness, difficult relationships are in many ways the*
> *most valuable for practice. The people who irritate us*
> *are the ones who inevitably blow our cover. Through*
> *them we might come to see our defenses very clearly.*
> —Pema Chödrön, *The Places That Scare You*

My daughter thinks I am a shithead.

I've been wallowing in self-pity again. It's been about a week. No writing. No late-night confessions to friends. No calls to the therapist or priestess. I haven't wanted to talk to anyone, haven't wanted to admit that I cannot deal with my daughter's thinking I am a shithead.

I mean, I honestly thought I was over my pathological self-doubting and weird need to please everyone. I am smart. I am confident. I'm Hip Mama for chrissake! *Why is this happening to me?*

My daughter has a new phrase: "Who's the genius?"

She says this every time I make a mistake. She also says this every time I do not make a mistake. She says it if I have a brilliant plan, a bright idea . . . anything. She says, "Who's the genius?" This is a rhetorical question. I make the wrong turn. *Who's the genius?* I think a pair of blue-and-white striped pajama pants look OK to wear grocery shopping. *Who's the genius?* I bought the really big bag of arugula. All right? I am *not* the genius. Why can't I deal with this? I have one teenage girl-child, and I might as well be in middle school for the loser I feel like.

My daughter thinks I am a shithead, and here's the recurring tangent my brain goes back on when she says so: Everything I have ever done has been a complete joke. Our house is ugly. I never made enough money. I never learned to cook. Imagine the mouth-watering childhood I could have given my daughter if I had only gone to the culinary academy instead of journalism school. Cooks make money, don't they? I could be flying all over the country, taking my daughter to visit all the Ivy League colleges she would one day attend instead of stashing five dollars a day in the weird Gen-X lunch box someone gave me for Christmas, pathetically trying to amass a couple thousand dollars so I can send her on a four-week study-abroad program to make up for the fact that she is *so* state-school-bound. I mean, I was going to send my kid to the college of her choosing! That was the plan. My daughter was not going to have to pick a major based on which classes didn't conflict with her work schedule. *God, what am I tripping about?* Money isn't that important to me. And there's nothing wrong with state school. But maybe trying to convince myself that money doesn't matter is just me trying to make excuses for being the embodiment of loser-mom. I should change the name of my zine from *Hip Mama* to *Loser Mama*. Maybe I should have forced myself to marry the last schmuck who asked me. Maybe I should have gotten a house in the suburbs and one of those big, boxy cars you can't park anywhere. Maybe all of this feminist, urban crap was just me being selfish. I mean, at least if we were some square suburban family, my daughter would be a punk and I could relate . . . secretly, of course.

It's the apologizing I swore off just last week. And, yes, I know better. Giving our children the versions of us that they say they want—the socially acceptable, cool (but not *too* cool) parents they can parade in front of their friends—will do them no real good. If we join the bull-shitters, how will our kids ever learn to be real? Still, when our sons and daughters become the messengers of the "you are unacceptable" we've heard all of our lives, it's hard not to internalize it.

I feel abandoned even though I know my daughter is *supposed* to abandon me at this point.

I was having a beer with my barely past-adolescence-friend the other day. I'd just done a reading from my new (adolescent) memoir.

She said, "Your reading, it was really kind of sick."

I frowned, took a sip from my bottle of Guinness. "Sick? How so?"

She nodded. "It was just really *sick,* if you think about it. Mad sick."

I said, "I thought it went well . . . the thing I read . . . I thought it was *funny* . . ."

And she nodded again, smiled. "Yeah. It was funny. And the whole thing was just seamless. It was sick. You know . . . awesome?"

I closed my eyes for a minute, opened them. "Sick means awesome?"

She took a sip of her beer, spoke more slowly this time. "Yeah. You know? Your reading? It was awesome."

The trickling stream of an age difference between us suddenly swelled into a raging river. All at once I realized: I am. Officially. An old fogy.

⟲   ⟲   ⟲

Now, I've been called a lot of things as a mother over the years: too poor, too young, too permissive, too strict, overbearing, negligent . . . on and on. But now my daughter seems to agree with the critics. She thinks I'm a shithead. She isn't hating me all the time. We're not at each other's throats. Take today. She actually kissed me on the cheek when I dropped her off at the mall. Kissed me! In front of her friends! Things are actually going pretty . . . *well*. So it's all the more mind-boggling to me that I'm having such a hard time with it. But I've spent my entire adult life up until now feeling like it was just me and my daughter against the world. I didn't mean to feel that way. I never thought to myself, *Hey, here's a healthy way to think about one's small family: embattled—us versus them.* It's just that so much of the world was so callous to my girl-child, and so callous to me. We fought that. We learned to fight that. I became her advocate. I became my own advocate. Through colleges and universities, through preschools and elementary schools, through family courts and toy stores, through the medical establishment and the rental ads, through this whole culture that disses mothers at every turn, I was the commander in chief of our two-girl army. And we survived. And we kept on surviving. We *thrived*. So, what does it mean now if my daughter thinks I'm a shithead? If she's questioning my authority? What does it mean when she says, Maybe the world was right all along? Does it mean it's just *me* against this "mad sick" world now? Does it mean I have to go to therapy to figure out what my freakin' problem is—why I see life as guerrilla warfare? Does it mean I have to lay down my arms? And if I do have to lay down my arms, is it because we won or because we lost?

◎   ◎   ◎

I had no answer for any of these questions, so I did what I've always done when confused: I asked the *I Ching*. And which oracle should I get but Revolution?

The Chinese character for this hexagram means, in its original form, molting or shedding skin. This is not a violent revolution. It's a transformation based on the passage of time. It's a complete rotation.

"Revolution," the *I Ching* told me, means "removal of that which is antiquated." According to the text, two daughters are in conflict, but the younger one has the upper hand. They "dwell together, but their views bar mutual understanding." Still, the reading was optimistic. "Give thought to altering the entire nature of the relationship," my book advised. "It will take time and effort . . . but success is definitely assured."

This improved my mood immeasurably. You can't go wrong with "success is assured"!

When my daughter takes me to task for every damn thing I do, I guess I can also take a little pride. I did not raise someone who would go through life unquestioning, someone who would follow orders without thought. When my daughter rebels against me, I guess it's also an opportunity for me to ease up on my own defensiveness, to take another look at who I am and what I believe.

As parents, we don't have to accept the shame or the "you're not good enough." We don't have to reinternalize all the societal stigmas we just barely got over. Teenage kids can be seriously mean to their parents. They hate us irrationally as they once loved us irrationally. We don't have to take what they say personally. But we can look at it. We can consider it. We can take the opportunity to see some of the ways in which we *are* shitheads.

I mean, did I really expect—or want—my daughter to grow up to *be* me? Let's face it, I've had a pretty hard time being me in this life. I can't know if her path will be easier, but I can admit that my worldview contains some antiquated nonsense.

As parents, we get to see our defenses very clearly now. We can learn to be more confident in the parts of ourselves that are real and awesome. And maybe we can shed some old skin, too.

Revolution.

Everything is turned upside down.

My young friend calls my reading "sick." And this is a compliment.

My daughter thinks I am a shithead. And maybe this is a good thing.

Who You're Gonna Get

Maia says, "When you thought about having a baby, did you think you would get . . . me?"

I say, "I'm glad I got you."

She says, "But how did you picture I'd be, you know, when I became a teenager?"

I say, "Well, I guess when I imagined it, I thought you would be more . . . like me."

She laughs. "Why?"

I say, "I don't know. When you picture your kids, don't you imagine them as little versions of yourself?"

She says, "Yeah, but more popular."

And I say, "Well, what if you get someone like me?"

She gasps. "A dork?!"

I say, "Yeah, I mean, it could happen."

And she's silent for a long time. Finally she sighs, "Someone. Like. You."

I say, "Yeah, a lot of times you get someone really different from yourself. Gammie got Nonna. And Nonna got me."

She interrupts me, saying, "And you got me. And I'm like Gammie! Do you think I'll get someone like Nonna?!"

I shrug. "Maybe. You might even get a boy."

This, however, is too much for her to fathom. She shakes her head, says, "No. I might get a girl like Nonna. But I am *not* going to get a boy."

The Hardest Thing about Being a Teenager

I asked fifteen- and sixteen-year-olds, "What's the hardest thing about being a teenager?"

Guys
Girls
Parents
Stereotypes
Judgment
Friends
Grades
Responsibilities
Finding direction
Growing up
No money
Mean teachers
Getting enough sleep
Following all the rules

I smoke myself retarded
Balancing life: school, work,
    friends, family
The constant nag of parents
Peer pressure
Trying to understand yourself and
    how you fit into society
Doing the right thing
Not getting the respect you deserve
Criticism from shallow people
Can't wait till adulthood
Realizing you aren't who
    you want to be
Being looked down on by adults
Living up to others' expectations
Getting what you want
Not getting what you want
Expectations shattered
Dealing with all the changes
    around you
Making the right choices
What's the hardest thing about being a
    teen? For me, it's independence. You
    really do love your parents, but you
    just want to do your own thing.
    When you're fifteen, sixteen, what-
    ever, you think you're all grown up
    and you know it all. So you want to
    make your own rules and live your

own life. But at the same time, you still want to be the little girl cuddling up with your mama when you're sick. It's hard to find the balance between adult and child, for both the parents and the kids.

A Chaos Theory
of Adolescence

Contrary to popular belief, most teens actually get along fairly amicably with their parents. In 2003's "State of Our Nation's Youth" survey, 75% of high schoolers said they got along "very well" or "extremely well" with their caregivers. There is no werewolf transformation from being a perfect, loving, beautiful child to being an uncontrollable, beastly teen. Your average two-year-old is a thousand times harder to manage than your average fifteen-year-old. It's just that life is changing. And change is hard. Remember the insanely intense culture shock when you first became a mom? You're still a mom, will always be, but these years are just as transformative as those early ones. We're leaving something that is known for something that is unknown. And it's time to hit those chaos theory books again. Because change hurts. Sometimes in a physical way. Chaos. The word brings to mind images of confusion and turmoil. But chaos theory doesn't teach us that the universe is without order. It just reminds us that the order is intricate, changeable, and, yes, unavoidable. All the little causes and effects, all the hormone shifts and rites of passage and astrological transits that seem insignificant in the short term can have spectacular effects in the long run. This quality is known as "extreme sensitivity to initial conditions." When a wild wind blows through the branches of a tree, there's no telling which leaves will fall—or where.

Chaos theory teaches us that phenomena that aren't predictable can't be optimized. In other words, there are no magic ten steps to a perfect life with our teenagers. All we can do, according to chaos theory, is increase our understanding of the chaotic phenomenon's nature—its properties, patterns, structure, and features. Chaos theory suggests that if we can understand some of the patterns of adolescence, it will be easier to wrap our brains around the apparent pandemonium of our daily lives. This is not the apocalypse, after all. It's just a life stage. Much of what is going on in our homes is going on in tens of millions of other homes at the same moments. Our children are redirecting and confirming their futures.

So let's look at the nature, patterns, structure, and features of adolescence: Our girls start out a few steps ahead, asking questions like *How do I fit in?* There's plenty of emerging sexual energy, and emotional emphasis is on relationships with peers. Even though seventh and eighth grade can be extremely difficult, kids often experience some grief over losing their middle school identities as they move into high school. Loneliness tastes like pennies. Kids want to find a niche. Homeschooled children sometimes enter school for the first time and have to learn to negotiate the almost overwhelming social drama. A new self-consciousness dawns for everyone.

As the "Who am I?" questions arise and get more intense, old family issues and events are revisited. Expect inquiries about the divorce or the death in the family or the move several years back.

There are a million decisions to be made: *How will I deal with schoolwork? Who will I hang out with? Party scene or no?*

Boys "bulk up." Girls start to get bodacious. Or they don't. Which is worse? Some kids develop dangerous relationships with food and body image—often most intense around sophomore year, according to health-care providers.

Old questions linger and new ones arise: *How do I relate to all these adults in my life? Do I give a shit about schoolwork? Are my friends good enough? Are they the right kind for me? Do I like myself? In what ways are my parents idiots? And when will I get my driver's license?!*

By junior year, the boys catch up with the girls—developmentally—and everyone starts to relax in each other's company. Just in time for the new big anxieties, like *What am I gonna do after high school?* Boredom settles like snow. The social scene leaves something to be desired. Closer friendships beckon. And serious experimentation is a way to keep life interesting. A stronger sense of self emerges as friendships change and deepen. Relationships with grownups shift at this point, too, as kids want to be seen as more responsible young adults.

Senior year is often comfortable socially—being the oldest on campus has its security. *But what about the future? I know who I am in this world of family and school, but who will I be in the larger world? Will I ever have as deep relationships with people as I had in high school? I'm just getting a handle on everything. I'm ready to go. I'm scared. I'll be leaving home. What will my relationship with my parents be like now?*

I have mixed feelings about all the newfangled scientific information on "the teen brain" (one should be suspicious of all brain-chemistry research, seeing as all the "scientific" reports seem to conclude with a big marketing plug for some new psycho-pharmaceutical drug from hell), but it's worth reviewing the data and taking from it anything that rings true or feels helpful.

Basically, the new research says that teenage brains simply don't function the same way that grownup brains do. This negates pre-1990s theories that the hundred billion neurons firing inside an adult's skull were already in place by the time a kid hit puberty. Now the scientists are saying that a teen brain is a work in progress, and one that develops in chaotic fits and starts. One of the very last areas of the brain to fully mature is, not surprisingly, the part we use to make sound decisions and calm ourselves down out of panic, despair, or rage. In some ways, teenage kids look like grownups but think like children. They aren't being flaky jerks as often as they might appear to be—they have a legitimately hard time organizing multiple tasks and grasping complex ideas.

Teen Suffers Burns after Setting Own Shorts on Fire

ELGIN, Ill., September 23, 2002—An Illinois teenager suffered second-degree burns during a game with two other boys where they would splash gasoline on their pants, set them on fire, then try to put them out.

Police said the boys took turns smearing their shorts with gasoline in the back yard of an Elgin home. They would then take turns lighting each other's pants on fire, and the teen whose pants were set on fire would drop to the ground and roll in an attempt to put the fire out.

After three rounds, police said, "the shorts were drenched in so much gasoline that they were unable to extinguish it anymore."

*A 16-year-old boy suffered second-degree burns from the
waist down. He was treated at a local hospital and released.*

*Police said none of the boys would be charged in the incident
because "being totally stupid is not a crime."*

The good news: If brains aren't fully formed until adulthood, teens still have a chance to develop restraint, clear judgment, a sense of right and wrong, and even empathy.

The new science blames moodiness not on weak character, but on teenage brains' underdeveloped ability to process emotions. Oversensitivity and fly-off-the-handle responses are blamed on a teen's inability to correctly read other people's emotions, to understand subtle social signals, and to interpret meanings.

The prefrontal cortex goes through a growth spurt around age ten or eleven—neurons start to sprout new connections—but around age twelve, most of those start to die off in a process called "pruning" that's supposed to ensure that the brain nourishes only useful connections. This process allows the brain to function more efficiently, but until it's done, kids don't have all the neuron power they need to make right-on decisions.

A tendency to take wild risks is compounded by other intricacies of brain chemistry: genetic traits that push us to leap without looking, the fact that thrill seeking stimulates the pleasure-pumping dopamine system, and a common adolescent decline in serotonin that makes impulse control tricky business.

While most kids experience a decline in serotonin production, kids whose brains make *too much* of the stuff can tend toward obsessiveness and perfectionism. Starving the body of the proteins it needs to make even more serotonin can make kids feel less anxious. Throw in the social pressure to be thin, and it's a perfect biochemical setup for anorexia.

Add sex hormones to all of this, and we're dealing not only with a blossoming interest in sexual expression but also with a total remodeling of the brain. Aggression, the likes of which we haven't seen since the toddler years, is not uncommon—only now, kids are big enough and resourceful enough to do some real damage.

So, do the brain chemists have anything comforting to tell us? Only that in spite of everything, most kids emerge from adolescence physically and emotionally intact.

Astrologists have a parallel take on what's going on through the teen years. Their measuring arcs are wholly different—planetary influences instead of neurons and chemicals—but their predictions are roughly the same: At age twelve, kids hit the "Jupiter return," a transit that has gotten decidedly less press than the infamous "Saturn return" of our late twenties, but is, apparently, an even bigger deal. Jupiter rules all things expansive—joy, movement, and the unknown—so the Jupiter return sets off a new growth cycle and a broadening of ideas about life, identity, and potential. Then around age fourteen—halfway to the adult Saturn return—comes the "Saturn opposition," which sets the stage for independence and separation. Responsibilities begin to weigh heavily; family problems can arise; and kids have to learn to deal with the people around them on a new, almost-adult level.

So we're in new territory. Again. And as parents, we haven't figured out where all the bogs and the leg traps are yet. It's easy to feel like our work is done at this point. Our kids say, "Leave me alone," and it's easy to take that as a broader directive than what they mean, which is probably something more like, "Leave me alone *right now.*" So there's a temptation to turn our backs entirely, not because we don't want to hang out with them, but because we feel unnecessary, used up, dated. I mean, who wants to hang out where she's not wanted?

Kids do need to be left alone sometimes, but they also need conversation, affirmation, even a little *direction.*

Through all the changes in mind, body, and world, here are our kids' basic tasks over the (roughly) seven years of adolescence:
- To gradually achieve independence
- To decide on/prepare for life's work
- To adjust to sexual maturation
- To establish meaningful relationships with friends
- To develop a sense of identity
- To strengthen, and begin to trust, intuition
- To accept new responsibilities/learn how to follow through
- To understand and deal with the values and beliefs of the larger community/society
- To puzzle about the meaning of life/develop a life philosophy

As my daughter enters adolescence, I'm entering my mid-thirties, so I'm still on the young side as the mom of a teenager. My brain is fully formed, but I'm changing, too. No matter how old we are, having a teenager around makes us feel our own age more powerfully. Our kids are constantly drawing our attention to the fact that we're out of fashion (and if we're not out of fashion, *how embarrassing,* we must be trying to act like teens!). If their grumblings aren't enough, there's reality: I could be a grandmother any year now. I go to bed before she does. And since I've only got the one kid, I have a level of freedom and independence I haven't seen in more than a decade. What *did* I used to do with my time? And when did I start looking like such a *grownup?* It's scary business in a youth-obsessed culture to one day look in the mirror and realize that this time train really isn't going to stop.

As parents, we've made huge emotional and financial investments, and suddenly whole childhoods have passed us by. Even if we've finally saved up enough money for that always-planned trip to the Carlsbad Caverns, our kids may not want to go. It's natural for us to grieve the loss of their younger presence in our lives, and to start to question some of the choices we've made. It's easy now to start projecting a certain disillusionment and pessimism about life—just when our kids need us to glow optimistic about *their* life plans.

Whether we're in our thirties, forties, fifties—whatever—when our kids hit their teen years, we're still growing and changing, too. Erik Erikson has mapped out a bunch of adult life stages, so as our kids enter high school, we're probably looking at "intimacy vs. isolation" (as in, *Do we have any intimate or deep relationships beyond those with our kids, or are we otherwise cut off from other human beings?)* or "generativity vs. stagnation" (as in, *Are we looking forward to manifesting our dreams in the world, or are we tripping on past failures and disillusionment?).*

Astrologically speaking, when we enter our forties, the planets have some intense and predictable midlife transitions planned for us as well, with struggles to realize personal dreams, a need to learn to collaborate fairly with others, and a focus on aligning radical ideas with social acceptance. Development. Change.

To fall into the traps of cynicism now would be a major bummer, because we've got a few developmental tasks of our own:

- To evaluate/rethink our careers or life work
- To stop whining about the past

- To achieve some level of financial stability
- To help our kids become adults
- To listen to our bodies and adjust to grown-up biological changes
- To develop a few deep friendships
- To deal with our new mentorship role in our work and communities
- To learn to use our newfound time
- To grow into the authority and wisdom of mid-adulthood

Our adult identities may have ended up getting built around having small children, so somewhere in all those tasks, too, we have to make the time and mental space to consider questions like *What does it mean to be a fully human grown-up mama-woman?* And:

> *Who am I*
> *Beyond*
> *My child's mother*
> *My mother's daughter*
> *My résumé's writer*
> *My lover's partner*
> *?*

So, we need to keep it real, to stay open and focused on the now, and the way the light comes in through the kitchen window, and the future, and all the truth of its possibility and promise. We can't succumb to the available bitterness or jadedness—the easy roads of emotional abandonment or blurry, rose-tinted hindsight. We'll have our doubts. We'll have our nostalgia. And we can live with those things without getting sucked into world-weariness. Chaos theory says that life is complicated. We don't have to imagine that everything will unfold in some predestined, linear forward motion. But we can study the patterns, structures, and common features of the storm. We can understand the tasks in front of us. And we can remember that cause and effect spiral in on themselves, that there's no telling where the leaves will fall. Later, looking back on these years, all we'll really want is to be able to say that we did our best not to be an asshole, did our best to embolden those around us, did our best to trust in the rhythm of experience.

Chemical Reactions between Hormones and Society

Adolescence is just one big walking pimple.

—Carol Burnett

Lies the Media Told Me

When I moved to Portland in 2000 and accepted a residency teaching creative writing at a public high school, friends and acquaintances called me "brave." The school I'd been assigned to was, they said, "one of the rough ones." I had no reason to doubt their judgments. They knew the city better than I did, after all. And I'd been watching the news. I understood that American high schools had become hotbeds of violence and turmoil. My own kid was only eleven. It had been years since I'd spent time with a real teenager. But news is news, and what are we gonna do but shake our heads and grumble, "Kids today . . ." and "I'll be damned . . ."

On my first visit to my new job site, I wasn't sure whether to feel reassured or terrified to discover an open campus with no metal detectors and very little visible security. A single uniformed official wandered down a cement path outside. Students and strangers alike could come and go as they pleased from the square brick building—with god-knows-what hidden in their backpacks.

Would I be jumped in the hallways? Would I be verbally assaulted with crude phrases I didn't know the meaning of? Would I be shot in the middle of a class? The newscasters wouldn't even act shocked when they reported my death. "Adding to the rising tide of senseless school violence," they'd say. And then cut to a commercial for laundry detergent.

I bit my lip. But a job is a job and I had rent to pay, so in I walked.

Empty halls, fluorescent light, peeling paint. I stood there for a moment, tried to imagine coming every day as a teacher, tried to imagine being a student within those walls. The place smelled vaguely of disinfectant.

When a bell rang, I took a deep breath.

A flood of kids poured out of classrooms, strutting and flirting, swearing and laughing, stylish and diverse.

"What's up, dawg?"

"Not much, man. You goin' to the game today?"

"Naw, gotta study for that test."

A symphony of lockers being opened and slammed.

A nauseating waft of Old Spice and sweat.

Then a friendly, pimpled face in front of mine: "Hey, are you a new student here?"

"Um, no." I shook my head. "I'm gonna be a teacher here starting next week."

Flush of embarrassment: "Oh, sorry. Well, hi."

Looks can be deceiving, I know. But these kids inspired no fear. *Weird,* I thought. *They actually seem kind of nice.*

Like I said: I watch the news. I read the papers. And even though I know paying too much attention to CNN can make a girl stupid, I found it hard to believe that my fear of teenagers was just another case of TV-inspired paranoia. But here I was, at an "inner-city" high school, and it felt more like the set of *Clueless* than a war zone.

⊚　　⊚　　⊚

In my daily paper, kid criminals get bold headlines while adult offenders barely make the police logs. The much-advertised "epidemic of youth violence" of the 1990s, coupled with forecasts about the growing teen population, prompted dire predictions for a generation of "super-predators." In a 1995 article in the *Weekly Standard,* Princeton professor John Dilulio envisioned "high-rate juvenile offenders coming at us in waves over the next several decades." And as if not to disappoint the terrified masses, the news media spent the next few years fueling these visions of teenagers running through the streets with guns and knives, high on crack, warring chaotic against innocent grownups on every corner.

Did the high school kids just *look* nice? Maybe they'd be lying in wait for me behind the building at lunch hour—wolves in sheep's clothing.

Where were these super-predators?

I was an A+ statistics student back at Mills College, so after my orientation meeting on campus, I decided to go to the city library and find out.

Well, I'll be damned. A quick study of the data revealed that teenagers commit just 13% of violent crimes. Including the Columbine shootings, there were only half as many violent deaths on campuses nationwide in the 1998–99 school year (twenty-five) as there were in the early 1990s (over fifty per year). That's right. While the massacre in Littleton, Colorado, was nothing short of horrifying, every newscaster who asserted in its aftermath that school violence was escalating lied. They lied.

Crime and violence exist—always have—but the news reports, it turns out, have blown the problem way out of proportion. There is no "rising tide." There is simply a tide. It ebbs and flows. The hype about teen crime has done little for public safety. Instead, it's contributed to a society in which young people are now held to higher standards than adults apply to themselves: Their constitutional rights are ignored; youth culture is targeted for censorship; and when teens do commit crimes, not only are they increasingly tried as adults, they're given harsher punishments than grownups. Offenders against children often receive the most lenient sentences.

So if kids aren't monsters, they must be victims, right?

It seems like whenever the news isn't reporting shocking crimes committed *by* young people, they're feeding parents' and children's fears with sensationalized reports of crimes *against* kids. Indeed, teenagers are more likely to be victims than assailants. But here's a fact that I've never seen reported on CNN: A teenager is now less likely to be the victim of a serious violent crime than at any time since Lyndon Johnson was president. That includes all the high-profile cases we've seen again and again on ABC, CBS, NBC, CNN, Fox News, MSNBC, and all the other all-fear-all-the-time networks.

Atrocities against children are real. Our grief blazes indescribable and deserves to be honored. Statistics are no solace when you or your child is the one who gets hurt, but while the news media love to convince us that the world is getting worse and worse—that surely the end of civilization is nigh—here's another reality: Back in 1900, fully 20% of kids lived in orphanages; and rates of alcohol abuse, drug abuse, and domestic violence were all significantly higher than they are now.

The golden era of the American family everyone seems so nostalgic for never existed. It *never* existed. It's a pie-in-the-sky, big patriarchal lie. And whether or not you believe in generalizations about generations, it is a fact that in recent years virtually every youth indicator has taken a turn for the positive. According to Neil Howe and William Strauss, authors of *Millennials Rising,* old clichés of teenage cynicism, angst, and alienation are giving way to a new confidence about the future, and—ironically—a new trust in parents and authority figures. Youth crime, school violence, suicide, and hard-drug-abuse rates are all declining. Measures of teen optimism, achievement, and sense of peer solidarity are all on the rise.

Comforted by my new knowledge, I felt guardedly optimistic as I headed back to campus for my first real day on the job. In a window-less classroom, I stood in front of thirty-two kids at their tiny desks and introduced myself. I smiled. A few kids smiled back. Some picked their noses. One appeared to turn *up* the volume on his CD Walkman. Five or six seemed preoccupied with counting the ceiling tiles. *Right,* I remembered. *My task here is to engage them, not obsess about which one of us is going to assault the other.*

And so I read them a Bukowski poem, and I asked them to write a poem of their own.

Pens flew across paper.

"Does anyone want to read what they came up with?"

A few hands rose.

I felt my body start to relax.

All times are dangerous times. But not every relationship has to be played out as a contest between monster and victim.

Over the course of my first six-week residency, and through three more years of high school teaching gigs, I met some disillusioned teens. I met some angry teens. I met some scared teens. But the vast majority of the teens I met were shockingly . . . *well-adjusted.* They were whole and real human beings who were sometimes frustrated, sometimes bored, sometimes unhappy, sometimes stoned, but usually doing just fine—shy and flirtatious, cool and guarded, sober and upbeat, well-spoken and funny. Sometimes my students wrote about violence at home and violence on the streets. But mostly they wrote about love and adventure, good grades and strict teachers, romance and sexuality, politics and music, ghosts and dreams, family vacations and "sneaking out." They wrote about their grandmothers' funerals and their nephews' births. They wrote about racial identity and mountain trails. They wrote about immigration and nostalgia for their childhoods.

And not one of them ever pulled a gun on me.

Gym Socks & Freedom

I asked fifteen- and sixteen-year-olds, "What does high school smell like?"

> Sweat
> Pencils
> Moldy books
> Gym socks
> Dust
> Flowers
> McDonald's
> Hormonally charged boys
> Soap
> Wet branches
> Chalk
> Stale food in lockers
> Cigarettes
> Freedom

Paper
Permanent marker
Wite-Out
A new coat
Burnt rubber from the radiator
Bento
Cologne and attitude
Pot
Leftovers
Cafeteria food
Real nasty
Beauty-concerned girls
A forest
Loneliness
High school smells like perfume. I
    hate it. Freshman hall smells like
    peaches. I also hate it.

"My Mom Had Trust in Me and My Decision"

Conventional wisdom tells us that dropping out of school is a cata-strophic event in any teenager's life. But high school isn't the only path to a soulful adulthood. Sometimes kids just need to take some time off to explore the larger world and find a renewed focus and enthusiasm for learning. I talked to David, a nineteen-year-old artist from Hunts Point in the Bronx, about his big decision.

Me: How would you describe your upbringing?
David: I grew up without a father, really. What I do remember of him [is that he] was abusive to my mother. So I grew up raised by my mother since the age of six, and she is the best and coolest thing in my life.

Me: Did your communication stay open through your teen years? Was there a time when you became more isolated from her?
David: I was and still am an artist. I don't think that she took it the wrong way. I wasn't interested in a lot of things other boys were so

that might have given a wrong impression, but I turned out fine. I just wanted time to explore myself as well as my mind.

Me: How much freedom did she give you to explore that?
David: It's not really the freedom that I got so much as the honesty. I was taught very well and received a lot of trust, which led to ultimate freedom. From there it just grew. I never had a reason to lie to my mother. She was even open-minded about pot smoking and drinking, because she taught me well enough not to be controlled by anyone or anything. She was proud of what I was and is proud of what I am becoming.

When I decided to leave school and take the GED, my mom had trust in me and my decision.

Me: What led up to that decision?
David: I had not seen any improvement or knowledge gained while I was in school. It was the same for me and all my friends. We were at an art school to improve on our talent and individual styles. The school art classes were so low caliber, it really caused more than half the students to hate art. I left because I felt my love and passion for art was slowly being depleted. I didn't want to lose myself for a sad excuse for an education.

Me: What did you do once you left school? I think people worry about "dropouts" because they think that's it for learning and growth—that teens will just go wild or head down some dead-end path.
David: I took time, and I listened to and experienced life. I got the most out of education from life experience. Even had very deep thoughts on the main four: science, math, historical studies, and

English. The world offered the same lesson: I just took the time and looked for it and it really made me grow up. Once you're on your own—without having the same group of friends and losing contact with the people you were around in school—so many paths do open up. A lot of those paths do lead to problems. It depends on the people that you spend the time out of school with. I became smarter and more worldly. It gave me the ultimate time to become a real man.

Me: What are you up to these days?
David: I'm now taking the time to finish off with school and go to a college of art, and I'm kinda falling in love, and things are going good now.

Survival Tactics

As I mentioned, an American teenager is now less likely to be the victim of a serious violent crime than at any time since the mid–1960s. This fact deserves further scrutiny. We need to understand *why*. A walk down the street with a teenager—with anyone who looks old enough to be humiliated and young enough not to fight back—can be alarming.

Three real-life scenarios that took place last weekend:

A thirteen-year-old girl who looks about sixteen and a thirty-six-year-old woman who looks about eighteen heading home after a concert in Portland. As soon as they part from the rock show crowd that's spilled out onto the sidewalk, the catcalls begin.

"Woo hoo!"

"Ow . . ."

"Hey, hotties!"

One man, leaning his head out his car window, actually

chooses to yell, "Show me your labia!"

A fourteen-year-old boy on his way to a convenience store two blocks from his house in San Francisco.

Two men in a red Chevy pull over and roll down their window. "Do you wanna make some money?"

The boy says he does not and assumes a ready stance.

"C'mon, man. We just need you to pick something up. What's your name?"

A woman pushing a stroller appears from around a corner.

The boy walks away with her to the store.

I hike along a rural road a mile from a popular lake resort in an Oregon forest. I'm wearing shorts and a tank top borrowed from my daughter. When I hear a car round the curve behind me, I step off to the side of the road.

Dude slows to a cruise, leans out his window, "Hey, baby."

I turn to him and stare, silent. I've got a rock in one pocket and a cell phone in the other, but my first line of defense is to show him that I am not a baby.

He apologizes and rolls on.

Three scenarios. Two children and two grown women home safe, but not because the level of aggression on the street seems diminished since the '70s, '80s, '90s.

Our kids are safer, but not because the world has grown friendlier. *Why, then?*

I think our kids are safer because of feminist and self-defense efforts like Home Alive, Model Mugging, and martial arts training. Our kids are safer because they are a lot less likely to be wandering the streets alone. With very few exceptions, the parents I talk to say that their children have less freedom than they did as teenagers.

To be fair to the mainstream media, our kids are safer partly because the nightly news puts the fear of god into all of us. When I interviewed teens for this book, virtually every white female I talked to said she'd been aware of "stranger danger" from an early age. However, several girls of color and about half of the boys claimed that they had never feared being kidnapped or otherwise victimized by a stranger. Why would they? Real statistics be damned, the national news reports almost exclusively on the murders and kidnappings of pale-skinned, female children.

It's debatable whether a sense of vulnerability is helpful or incapacitating when it comes to personal safety. Fear that's not followed up with some kind of self-defense training can be disempowering, but many of our children *are* armed with the tools of awareness, the buddy system, martial arts, rocks, cell phones, and—sadly—mistrust.

"Why the woman pushing a stroller?" I asked my fourteen-year-old aikido-trained San Francisco friend when his mom told me the story.

He shrugged. "If everyone's a stranger, you should choose the mom, the cop, or the shopkeeper."

"Who taught you that?"

"I don't know," he shrugged again.

But someone taught him—so long ago that his response was practically instinctual.

All of this safety has a price, of course. When children and teenagers are constantly supervised, they miss out on a rich kid culture that can only flourish outside the watchful gaze of grownups. And they miss out on the life-skills lessons that can only be learned by being stranded at a train station in the middle of the night and having to figure out how to get home. Television can end up taking the place of old-school playground social lives. Structured afternoon and weekend activities can become the only alternative to isolation. You hardly ever see a kid with a house key around her neck anymore. And ain't that America: all gated communities and paranoia and "freedom" to duct tape ourselves into our homes. And ain't that parenting: my anarchistic values butting up against my fears and my awareness at every turn.

When a young woman in my community was murdered while thumbing rides across the state earlier this summer, my first reaction blamed the victim: "Why was she hitchhiking alone?" The possibility of being raped and killed should not dictate her travels. My second reaction was both a more disturbing question and a more philosophical one: "Why do men kill?" This is an urgent question for the world to answer and address. In the meantime, however, we are forced to be realists. We live in a violent culture. We are not free to travel safely as we please.

And so we counter with survival tactics. My daughter earns her freedom with darker- and darker-colored martial arts belts. The buddy system is all but compulsory. The cell phone is charged.

I'm no fool. I know that life is not safe. Heartening statistics and realist survival tactics do not guarantee anything. I envision and work toward a world in which men do not kill. But I am living here and now, parenting here and now.

My Parents Are Always Worried

I asked a group of teenagers, "Do parents worry too much?"

It's a normal thing for your parents to worry about you, but only to a certain extent. It's great that your parents care about you and your safety, but it's also very important for them to trust you. If they don't let you out to experience things, you won't be able to learn from your own mistakes.

—Camille, 17

My parents are worried about my safety to the point of annoyance. Due to their worries, I can't stay out late or go to parties. At home I can stay up as late as I want, but somewhere else is a whole other deal. I can understand my parents not wanting me wandering around at night with my friends, but my parents have gotten to the point where I swear they think I'm six years old. However, I'm six-foot, 200 pounds, lift weights, and play football. How many people would like to get involved in a violent way with someone like me? I'm all for being safe, but enough is enough. What will they do when I go to college?

—Geoffrey, 16

Moms are too protective of their children. They jump to conclusions about what you have been doing. They worry endlessly about where you are. I understand that they care for us, but someday they will have to let us go. It could be that they won't accept that their kids are changing and growing into young adults.

—"Girl," 18

I always feel safe when I'm outside of my house or just away from my grandparents. I'm never really alone, so in case something pops off, my boys got my back. The way parents could help their kids feel safe is to be in their personal business—but not so much to make them feel like you're invading their privacy. Just know who they're with and where they are.

—John, 17

Teenagers are like stoplights, always changing. Parents should always keep a close eye on their kids because they are probably being offered drugs or alcohol. You can punish and ground them, but the thing kids need above all else is love and support.

—Warren, 15

A Color-Coded Path to Independence

When Maia was eleven, we signed her up for tae kwon do.

Master Dan told us that if she worked hard, she could earn her black belt in about five years.

Five years. A mother's mind begins to calculate. Sixteen. At the youngest. White. Yellow. Green. Blue. Red. Brown. And, finally . . . black.

For fifty dollars a month that I couldn't really afford but could (technically) pay, Master Dan had handed me a color-coded plan for the years to come.

Tae kwon do can be fun. The exercise is important, too. But as far as I'm concerned, martial arts training has never been just another afterschool activity.

When Maia's requests for more freedom started, I had long since contrived my color-coded responses:

"Mom, when can I go to the park just with my friends?"

"When you have your yellow belt."

"Mom, when can I go to the corner store by myself?"

"When you have your green belt."

"Mom, when can I baby-sit?"

"When you have your blue belt."

"Mom, when can I ride the city bus?"

"When you have your red belt."

"Mom, when can I be out with friends after dark?"

"When you have your brown belt."

"Mom, when can I drive a car?"

"When you have your black belt. I might even buy you a Volvo."

"Mom, when can I do whatever I please?"

"When you have your black belt *and* have graduated from a self-defense program like Model Mugging."

The specific stages of freedom, and the math, are somewhat arbitrary. Our kids' level of responsibility, our own comfort levels, and community standards can and should come into play when delineating acceptable behavior. And I'm a believer in erring on the side of the mother hen. But our diminishing power over our kids is a real thing. Instead of simply dreading the day when they walk out the door and we can't chase them down, get them in a head lock, drag them back, and put them on a "time out," we can consciously and systematically prepare them.

If your kid hasn't had any martial arts training, start now. If they don't want to do it, bribe them with their freedoms. If your kid is already in martial arts, add a short self-defense course to the plan. Take the class with them. Street violence often includes manipulation or weaponry our kids can't defend against with traditional martial arts or hand-to-hand combat. When Maia had her yellow belt and medaled in a national championship, I knew she would always be able to hold her own against someone of her approximate size who tried to punch her out. But what about smarmy sweet-talking Joe? What about the guy with a gun? Her beautiful forms and studied sparring techniques would only get her so far. Model Mugging can be completed in a season and teaches practical self-defense and de-escalation techniques.

I was raped by an acquaintance when I was sixteen years old. I met him in an alley, but I followed him to his "party." He was bigger than me. He was stronger than me. I believed him to be armed. But I willingly followed him. And later, I did not scream. I was clueless, and then I was scared. Does this make it my fault? No. Did it have to happen? Probably not. One moment of consulting my intuition. One self-defense maneuver. One well-timed scream. That's all it would have taken.

Would Model Mugging have spared me the experience-trauma-guilt-memory? Maybe yes, maybe no.

Will Maia use her training if she ever needs it? Maybe yes, maybe no.

As a grandmother in Isabel Allende's novel *City of the Beasts* says, "Experience is what you learned just after you needed it." Colored belts can't always make up for lack of experience.

But when this final question arose, "Mom, can I quit tae kwon do?" I'd long since contrived my response: "Hell, no."

Critical Mass

It's not your imagination: There are a whole lot of kids coming of age in America right now. Malls overflow with pubescent shoppers and hanger-outers. High schools are crammed to capacity. Pop culture is all about teens and "tweens." And why wouldn't it be? Our kids belong to the biggest generational market since the postwar boomers.

Born during their own boom, which peaked in the early '90s, the "Millennial Generation" is some seventy-seven million strong—more than three times the size of Generation X. The most racially diverse group of teens in American history, Millennials are also the first generation large enough to create a critical mass. The sheer number of them has spawned a vibrant youth culture that is at turns exciting (kid-driven youth power!) and frightening (mogul-driven marketing madness).

"It's Totally Raining Teens!" a summer cover line on *Vanity Fair* proclaimed. And it's true. Every other Hollywood blockbuster is aimed at youngsters. Celebrity ranks teem with adolescent stars. And every time I go to the grocery store, it seems like there's some new glossy on the rack to give *Seventeen* and *YM* a run for their money: *Teen People,*

Teen Vogue, Teen Romance, Cosmo Girl, Elle Girl . . . Whatever Girl, Just Give Us Your Money, Girl!

Vanity Fair calls this generation "the most style-conscious, splurged-upon, and media-immersed army of ragamuffins in history." Not compliments, exactly, but a far cry from the "super-predators" we were warned about when our kids started kindergarten.

"Super-consumers" is more like it. At least that's what they become when the marketers have their way. Raised by baby boomers and Gen Xers who often encouraged them to participate in family decisions, and exposed to media and advertising from all sides, our kids became active, sophisticated consumers when they were very young.

And the merchants of pop culture know it.

In *Branded: The Buying and Selling of Teenagers,* author Alissa Quart notes that U.S. teens spend over $150 billion in "discretionary income" every year, buying clothes, CDs, and makeup. Much of this cash is earned by us, their parents, but since the kids are the ones spending it—or seriously influencing our spending—they've become the most-studied generation in history. Marketers employ "culture spies" to circulate among teens and find out what's hot and what's not. In focus groups, our kids are paid to empty the contents of their brains and to enlighten marketers on their tastes and opinions, likes and dislikes, and reactions to various branding campaigns. If your family has fallen prey to those campaigns, you've noticed, for example, that you buy Sprite instead of 7-Up when given the choice. Coca-Cola's lemon-lime soda started endorsing hip-hop icons in the '90s and managed to become the Millennials' first choice in "cool" soft-drink refreshment. It's one of the things that happens in a capitalist culture in which neither government grants nor fans are willing to support new artists:

Corporations come in and brand everything from our dissent to our joy. And with a generation so affluent and influential, the corporations can't seem to resist. Every organic, kid-sparked trend is almost immediately snatched up by the super-capitalists, repackaged, and sold back to them like it was Disney's idea to begin with.

The teen pop world comes complete with its own idols, as well. There's no real shortage of boy heroes (take Harry Potter), or male hip-hop successes (take Eminem). And there's certainly no shortage of exploitative images of young women. But it's "girl power" that has driven Millennial culture and differentiated it from the last major media lunge into the teen scene, the one that brought us Marlon Brando in *The Wild One* and James Dean in *Rebel without a Cause*. Virtually all of the megastars of entertainment aimed at today's teens are women: J.Lo, Britney Spears, Mandy Moore, Hillary Duff, Amanda Bynes, Beyoncé Knowles, and the reigning queens of teen-genre everything, twin moguls Mary-Kate and Ashley Olsen, the squeaky-clean sisters who got their acting start as babies on the sitcom *Full House*.

In movies—from the ridiculous *Legally Blonde* to Drew Barrymore's sexy-fun *Charlie's Angels* to the enlivening *Bend It Like Beckham*—cute boys are nothing more than the trophies for young, female heroes who crusade to criminalize animal testing, kick ass, and excel at sports.

All this "go-girl" spirit is of course a rip-off and a watered-down corporate version of Grandma's feminism and Mom's riot-grrl movement, but it's also an indication of real cultural change. The number of girls and people of color in student government at the middle school, high school, and college levels is unprecedented. Yep, there's another reality emerging with this massive generation—and it exists beyond capitalist markets. According to Howe and Strauss in *Millennials*

Rising, our kids belong to the most female-dominated and least race-conscious generation in U.S. history, and "the first youth generation in living memory to be actually *less* violent, vulgar, and sexually charged than the pop culture adults are producing for them." Two-thirds of today's high school students say they are offended by the sexuality of the media.

"It took a village. We're raised. Watch out," proclaims a headline on millennialpolitics.com, the website for the *Millennial Manifesto,* a youth-created product of over a thousand interviews and dozens of contributing writers. Manifesto authors claim that "Unlike our Gen X siblings, we will get involved and vote. We will not sit by and watch CEOs get rich at the expense of temporary workers; we will unionize. Unlike our Boomer parents who drive SUVs and pay lip service to protecting the environment, we will buy hybrid cars to fight the causes of global warming. Unlike our elder political leaders, we will not take big money from teacher's unions and simultaneously claim to be reforming education. . . . We see the world through new eyes and it is time everyone else started paying attention."

And they're probably right. Youth movements are nothing new, but there are so damn many of *these* kids that any semblance of unity among them will certainly bring about sweeping societal change. One hundred fifty billion dollars a year might rule the pop market, but imagine the effect even a modest number of Millennial voters could have in an upcoming election. Gen Xers tried to rock the vote, but even if we had shown up at the polls in real numbers, we couldn't have provided a majority for any one candidate or proposition.

By 2008, a critical mass of Millennials will be eligible to cast ballots, and as long as Jeb Bush isn't in charge of counting those votes, our kids will have the power to send the aging white boys who run the

American political scene packing.

According to Howe and Strauss's readings of the statistics, our kids will indeed rebel, but "they will rebel against the culture by cleaning it up, rebel against political cynicism by touting trust, rebel against individualism by stressing teamwork, rebel against adult pessimism by being upbeat, and rebel against social ennui by actually going out and getting a few things done."

Forgetting

Remember how it was to be young. Remember that the teen years are a period of intense personal growth and discovery. Remember that mistakes are normal, even necessary, and that you learn so much more from your own than from your parents'.

—Ben, 16

Do not forget that you, too, were once a teenager.

—Tisha, 15

I think the hardest thing about my kids getting older is that I do remember myself at that age. I am scared for them.

—Mama Clarissa

When I asked teens to give advice to parents, the most common response I got was "Listen!" But the second most common response was, "Remember your own teen years."

This made sense to me. I'd just finished writing a teenage memoir, so I felt good about having spent several years combing through memories. I was ahead of the game. I figured most problems between teens and grownups boil down to lack of empathy. And the key to empathy is memory, right?

About a year later, I happened to ask my friend China, an awesome mama of a sixteen-year-old, to tell me about her own adolescence. Her answer took me by surprise: "It's hard for me to remember being a teenager right now," she said. "I don't often think about it. I know teenagehood was the hardest time. I was sometimes suicidal, dropped out of school at fifteen, grasping to find a way to live in this world that was true to myself, became agoraphobic for two years, didn't really fully snap out of it until I went to Europe when I was eighteen. But I've had to distance myself from those memories. When I was full of my own teenage memories, I was a worse parent. I projected onto my daughter. I wanted to help her. But she is not me. I thought I knew that already, but I learned it once more. She was very opposed and shitty to me until I learned how to detach."

Far out, I thought. Was there a potential trap in that second piece of advice?

I had to admit that my freshly recovered, mined, and examined memories were doing me absolutely no good in my current mothering life. More than insight, they offered me anxiety. *Would my daughter have as difficult a journey?*

Now that China mentioned it, my memories did seem to encourage projection and "do it this way because I wish I'd done it this way" thinking. Or "let's talk about this problem you're having because when I used to get that look on my face, it meant that I was having a problem, and I always wondered what would have happened if my parents had asked about it" thinking.

I'd just been talking to another friend, the mother of an eighteen-year-old. This friend is irate, admittedly jealous, and stuck in a deep conflict with her kid. Most of the people around the family see this kid as immature, but basically well-adjusted and ambitious. Doing just fine. But the mother keeps saying things like "When I was that age, I had three jobs," and "When I was that age, I was forced to get married," and on and on. So I was intrigued by China's idea. What would it be like for my friend to distance herself from her own memories?

China said, "I stepped through the looking glass when I became a parent of a teen. I'm on the other side now. Sometimes I see that parents are right and kids are wrong. I struggle with new dilemmas—remembering how it looked as a kid but also seeing a new viewpoint as a parent. It's like I can look out of two pairs of eyes. Even if I feel something my daughter is doing is wrong, that does not mean I can stop her or easily control her behavior. I experiment with how to handle problems. Some I never have fixed. Some she grew out of. But by detaching from myself as the teen, I feel born anew—no longer stuck in the past, discovering things fresh every day. People say I look young and act young for my age—they are always shocked that I have a teenager. But part of this "youthful" attitude is forgetting a lot of my own teenage-hood. I've internalized the lessons, and I remember it like any other time in my life, but it is not such powerful stuff to me anymore. My daughter is being the teenager now, not me. So I defer to her."

To forget.

To defer.

Something in China's words harkened back to the *I Ching* reading I got when I couldn't deal with the fact that Maia thought I was a shithead. The oracle described two daughters living in the same house—

they are in conflict, but the younger one has the upper hand. And it occurs to me that a huge part of my struggle is based on my own denial and my own reluctance to become an elder. I may not be an old woman, but I am Maia's elder. We are *not* two daughters living in the same house: We are mother and daughter.

I remember back to the day Maia told me she wanted to be a cheerleader, and when she told me she wanted to change the spelling of her name from M-a-i-a to M-y-a (that one lasted only a year). I remember the way those things stung when I first heard them, and the way I laughed at myself for resisting, but still felt depressed. It wasn't until I started hearing from friends and acquaintances who said things like, "I'm so sorry this is happening to you," and "I'm sure it's just a stage," and "Oh my god, how *horrible* for you—that was the name that you gave her!" that I realized how selfish and pathetic it was for me to make a stink about such personal decisions. I stood up for Maia instinctively, saying, "If she wants to call herself Cappuccino, that's up to her" and "Look, it's just *cheerleading*. She's not hurting anybody." And then I remember that my friend Krystee—a tattooed, radical, feminist, pagan dyke, if you don't mind labels—was the first one, when Maia told her about the cheerleading, to beam and congratulate and offer to help raise money for the uniform. And I remember how important that was. And how important it was a few months later when Inga moved to town and wanted to go with me to a game and see Maia perform. And the way all of that helped me to see and realize so clearly that these choices of Maia's were not even close to catastrophes. And now that China mentioned it, maybe that whole process boiled down to forgetting, to deferring, to withholding my projections, to letting go and saying, *Right on, Maia*. Because this isn't about my inner teenager. Maia is the teenager now. And she is not me.

It's a powerful exercise, this forgetting. China isn't talking about blocking out the past and making secrets of it. She's not talking about erasing memories. She says, "I've internalized the lessons, and I remember it like any other time in my life, but it is not such powerful stuff to me anymore." She's talking about laying the emotions *around* the memories to rest. She's talking about the internal change that allows us to move from projection to real empathy.

Empathy means understanding and entering into another person's feelings. Projection is attributing one's *own* feelings or experiences to another. Projection is a kind of bullshit empathy, but it's fairly easy to recognize if we're paying attention. When our thoughts or comments are prefaced by phrases like "God, when I was your age . . ." or "If I had it to do over, I . . ." what follows is probably not going to be empathetic. Our kids are not us. The good news is that *because* they are not us, they are *not* going to repeat our mistakes. They'll go through their own learning processes, to be sure. But having a teenager isn't a parent's second chance at getting her own adolescent initiation right. If we've got old business we're still tripping on, we can retrace our childhood and teen years and retrieve left-behind energy *for ourselves.* Our children cannot do that for us. And no matter what our relationship to our own youth, we can look in the mirror and see we are not sixteen anymore. And we can willfully stop obsessing about the past and live in the present—creating new experiences and discovering the world fresh every day.

A Day in the Life

Maia Swift

Early morning: The dream.

The dream's great! Always magical, never too much sex, too many fights, or sobbing, even though I always wake with a salty puddle upon my pillow and a stuffy nose. The noise of my alarm clock always finds a way to screech out of the mouth of the hot guy I'm dreaming of, as if it were part of the fantasy. So, naturally, I bash the guy on the top of his head to give me "just five more minutes" so I can finish the dream, and still wake much too early, in my opinion.

Still half asleep: Beautification process.

The beautification process includes brushing my hair so much I'm pretty sure it's unhealthy (I'm probably known at school as the girl who "should be balding right about now"!).

Finding the right outfit for how I think the day's going to end is tricky (maybe I'm the only one who does this?), but mainly I guess. The day usually ends how I figured it would (not a kind of "figuring" because it always ends the same way), but believing the day will end a certain way helps me get through it. The shower, hair, makeup, etc. match the outfit—not a desire, but the outfit gives off ideas that come naturally. I'm not entirely that way—sure, I'm a prep, but I'm not obsessed with the way I look, and I certainly don't think I'm hot shit, but I have to at least try and be all that my lacking-self-confidence-self raises me to be.

On my way out the door: School supplies.

I'm not the most organized girl, even though I try and change my approach every month or so. I gather up my homework, loose pens, books, signed parent notices, and makeup, and get on my way out the door. If transportation is up to my mom, it takes a li'l longer to get out the door—maybe a lot! Up to me? *P-e-r-f-e-c-t-l-y* on time. And with a friend? Time doesn't matter.

Around the time I'd usually sleep in 'til if I had my way: Before the first bell.

I meet up with my girls, my boy, or whoever "needs to talk *right away!!*"—I get the information I need for being caught up on the rest of the day, or I give it out. As the bell rings, I cram my way through the doors with the rest of my student body and watch as the stoners pile out of their corner, the couples out of theirs, and the guys who trade Yu-Gi-Oh! cards out of theirs. I smile at how everyone is so selectively put into groups—as if someone couldn't handle the "everyone's unique" speech, and *had* to shove them together.

First half of the day: Just getting warmed up.

I sit in every class, day after day, but I'm never bored. There's *still* that boy across the room that I wrote a letter to last night. I spent all night on it, but still it only says "What's up??" And it's perfect! If only he would give a signal—"Pass it to me!!"

Then there's my friend's drama—it happens every day, but not enough to call her at the least a "drama queen."

I don't understand why almost everyone breaks up in the first half of the school day. They know they'll have a hard day ahead of them. It would be so much easier to do it right before that last bell.

Midday: Lunchtime.

I fall into my group at our table, cheer up Krista, who's sad because her diet soda is getting warm. We chat about what teacher we know for a fact is having a pop quiz, and which one just got divorced from her husband, so "don't worry about that homework you didn't finish last night," and also "we have to go pick her up some you're-still-sexy lotion and a flower."

It's great giving teachers presents because you get that "you're the sweetest thing!!" look, and then, sometimes, no, more than sometimes, they start crying as if no other student's ever given them a present, and that they're so glad they went into teaching because they "just love kids," but it's such an "oh my gosh, that world peace stuff worked this time" cry.

Second half of the day: Just breaking down/in.

This is the time I find out who broke up with who, who's still with who, who's now with who, and who's going crazy because they didn't get to smoke out at lunch (and you can tell because they're freaking out). And . . . where's Tracy??

Kira hands me a folded note. It's a permission slip, the one we're supposed to turn in today, but it's blank.

"You have much better handwriting than me!!" she says.

A-rr-iii-ee-l G-ooo-rr-e I say to myself as I write with my new black pen. "Shit," I say, scrunching up my face. "That's *my* mom's name." I rip out a piece of paper from my notebook, in cursive I write, *Kira Reynolds is staying with our family this week, responsibilities are with me. Kira has permission to join this activity—Ariel Gore.* "Whatever," I mumble. "It'll work."

After school: More learning.

I run home and change into my cheer shorts, a tank, and grab my pompoms. I meet up with the rest of my girls and we walk to the track. We run laps, stretch, and learn new stunts, jumps, and cheers.

"Go, go, *g-o*. Go team go!!" We all chant.

I love cheerleading, and once you're in it, it's not about the boys, or even the sport, it's like a group of girls you can relate to, it's a big ol' slumber party!! It's fun, something I'm good at. Cheering is a life of its own.

After practice I meet up with Marie to talk, then head over to Italian lessons.

"*L'Italia é uno dei paesi piú belli del'Europa.*" I repeat after my teacher. Italy is one of the most beautiful countries in Europe.

After Italian, I get a bite to eat, and head home.

Evening: Homework.

I go to my room and dump all my homework on my desk. I sort it and do it in order of my classes—makes it easier for me. Also, if I do my early classes first, and I get too tired to finish my midday classes, I can always finish up during lunch, or in the library. Math, writing, reading, science . . . ugh, my fingers ache.

Marie usually calls around this time—"ring, ring . . ."

"Hey, what's up??" I answer cheerfully.

Marie and I talk about whatever for hours, what else happened since we last spoke, and "What are the answers for two through twelve??"

Later: Dinnertime.

Dinner's nice I guess, whether we go out for Chinese or Mom makes more pasta—not always pasta, but usually. She didn't used to know how to cook anything but pasta, and all the sauces were store-bought. I don't know what happened. We don't sit at the table, either, we're not really like that. I'd like to be that kind of family though, a lot, and sometimes Mom tries to have a nice family dinner around the table.

"Why don't we sit at the table tonight??" she says.

But I never did when I was little, so it doesn't feel right. When we go to my grandma's or great-grandma's house we sit at the table for a long time, and I always feel I'm saying, "May I please be excused??" at the wrong time, but I've never heard anyone ever say that I couldn't be.

And finally: Bedtime.

I don't really have a bedtime. Mom goes to bed way before me. I brush my hair, wash my face, all that. I can't stand falling asleep. By myself, in my own house, is the hardest. I think a lot at night. I wait around, just lie there, sometimes talk to friends on the phone or online, but they have to go to sleep at some point.

After a long while I slowly fall asleep, and wake up shortly after, way too early, to the dream.

Calling the Experts

Listen without judging. So many parents say they listen, but they really don't. All they hear is the bad stuff, not why or how the child feels.

—Henry, 15

The closest thing to an expert on "teen life" is, of course, a teenager. And even though none can speak for all, reading kids' poems, essays, and zines has given me a thousand times more compassion and insight into their inner lives than perusing teen magazines, watching MTV, reading parenting books, or, oddly enough, listening to my own child.

To *listen*. Teens and veteran parents alike tell me that that's the key to this whole stage. To *listen*. It seems so simple. But even a relatively quiet girl like myself—and one who is generally a good listener—has trouble. Here is my baby standing in front of me, telling me a story, telling me about her day, telling me about a problem. If I can bite my tongue and keep myself from jumping in to offer her unasked-for advice, if I can keep myself from telling her/showing her how to proceed the same way I told her/showed her how to tie her shoes, I'm doing pretty well. But even then, I'm focused on restraint. I'm not focused on the real and deceptively simple task before me: to *listen*.

I care almost instinctively for anyone I see as "somebody's child," but the fact that a teenager is not *my* offspring makes all the difference. There's perspective in emotional distance. I can listen to them. I can relate to them as I relate to any fellow human being. I can gain insight into and through them, and I can use that insight when I'm with my own family.

My daughter says, "When someone has a kid, they don't understand things the same way anymore." And I think that's especially true in relationship to our own children. We love them too much, we've invested too much as caregivers, we're too accustomed to telling them things and showing them how to do things. We've spent too many years obsessing and stressing over every fall, every potential scar. We've developed the nasty habit of seeing our kids as little versions of ourselves—and if they are just smaller, younger versions of us, why would we listen? We'd already know.

When I was in middle school, there was a teen hotline run by and for kids. We could call and anonymously ask our peers for support or advice. Wouldn't it be awesome if there was a teen hotline for the parents of teenagers to call? We could, anonymously, ask other kids what the hell was going on. We could use the distance of anonymity and no blood ties to gain a little perspective. Or we could just relax in an exchange that isn't burdened by the immense weight we attach to our parent-child relationships.

Sometimes, when I'm home alone, a friend of Maia's will pop up on my computer screen through instant messaging. The kid is trying to contact Maia, of course. But sometimes, even after they find out it's just me, we'll start to chat. It's open and *Hey, how's it going?* I'm reminded that the tension that sometimes exists between Maia and me isn't intrinsic to a teen-adult relationship, and I'm once again filled with gratitude for my friends who are also Maia's friends, who take her out to the movies or to the mall and give her a chance to hang out with a grownup who's not her mother, and whose brain isn't cluttered with real and imagined responsibilities or haunted by thoughts like *This has to be quality time,* or *Here's an opportunity for a lesson . . .*

I'm learning not to do that so much. In the meantime, I turn to other teenagers, to kids who can speak openly to me because I'm *not* their mother, and who I can, in some ways, more clearly *hear* because they are not my babies. So I'd like to dedicate the next couple of pages to the voices of those teenagers, speaking not to their parents but to other adults, to each other, and to themselves. Describing their inner lives, and what it means to be growing up here and now:

From the zine *Three Normal Guys,* by Justin, Micah, and James:

> *We are three inner-city youth trying to make it through the day.*
> *In the reading to come you are going to get a little insight to*
> *what's going on in our puny little minds. Some of it may not*
> *make sense to you but we don't really care because sometimes we*
> *don't even make sense to ourselves. We write about what's on our*
> *mind [and] it can be any subject from love to drugs so be*
> *prepared because our minds are not as simple as one may think.*

From the picture poem *Imagination,* by Marie:

> *Imagination hides under the bed, My Little Ponies carefully*
> *stored in a box, their stable with the matching fence is in the box*

next to it. The dollhouse that looks like a book is under there, too. The paper dolls have long since been lost. Shiny green silk, delicate lace, and tall pointy hats all crammed together in a mish mash of princess fairies and evil witches. Little hands grab at all of these, disrupting the dust and reopening the sticky lids.

From the zine *Rough Draft,* by Andrew:

I'm a pretty casual guy. I try to "embrace each moment" as much as possible. I like finding beauty, peace, self-understanding/ preservation in, well, "life." I like to think. I like to try new things; push my boundaries . . . but I enjoy thoroughly exploring different aspects of life as well. I often find myself dragging behind my racing mind, thinking about perspectives and viewpoints & different realities . . . subjectivity vs. objectivity/ objectivity vs. subjectivity. Maybe I'm uncontrollably hungry for food for thought . . . Maybe I'm just a wondering teenager (wandering traveler?) . . . Whatever I am (How to define . . . & why?), I like to sit and ponder. Some would call this a "thirst for life" . . . and maybe it is. I guess I just think (period) that, as cliché as it sounds, life is quite short: So I might as well hang/ party/rock on/live/experience/enjoy while it's around . . . while I'm around for it. Some also say this is a little "unusual" view for a teenager. I dunno. I went through a calming change in freshman (last) year. I used to think quite negatively . . . Not really enjoyable . . . Had some "bad" times, now I don't. And now it's time for "good" times. Yowza.

From the essay "Change," by Diane:

Just once I'd like to be someone else . . . Maybe, by being someone else, I could finally understand why they don't care. Why they never have any problems or worries. How they can forget about the Spanish assignment and not be frantically trying to finish it before the bell. I wonder if they think about the world the way I do, if they try to grasp their future as it floats by in a daydream. Do they know where they're going to be in ten years? Looking at them, I see the epitome of happiness, but do they just hide everything else away? Do they really struggle with the same insecurities and problems that I face seemingly alone? If I became someone else, would that allow me to escape myself, or would it just be a chance to understand that even those I could never relate to might have similarities I would never bring myself to acknowledge? Truly, there is no greater shortcoming in any of our minds; the idea that we try so hard to understand and empathize with others when honestly, we are all fake.

From the zine *Sometimes I Just Stop Thinking,* by Maeve:

I tend to avoid anything that makes me unhappy at all costs. Surprisingly, this does not result in happiness. It results in failed classes and broken promises and feelings color coded and filed away and never spoken out loud. . . . I like to think that by the time I am 28, all of the problems that I have now will have gone away, and that I might have new problems and maybe they will be bigger and more important, but won't hurt me so much. I like to think that all my problems are a direct result of being 15. This makes them seem less real and all something else's fault. They are chemical reactions between hormones and society.

What to Tell Your Kids about Sex

I asked parents, "What do you tell your kids about sex?"

I don't trip. We talk about sex at the dinner table. They were grossed out when I talked to them about oral sex, my youngest was perhaps eight at the time; my oldest, shocked, said, "Mommy! They don't need to know that!" I insisted that they did and from me. When my son was twelve, I told him about condoms, and again at the dinner table in front of his sisters. I talk about sex openly with my children. Anything they ask me I answer with candor, including about my own sex life. But I tell them that sex is not just enjoyable, and that it should be enjoyed, but that it should only occur with someone they feel deeply about and when they are emotionally ready. I also say that often we think we are ready because of urges we get, but aren't emotionally ready. I told them I didn't have sex until I completed high school, and recommend that they should consider waiting until then! I caution them about being careful, always protecting their health, of being sure how they feel about the person they might be considering having sex with.

*When my oldest had sex, I had talked to her about how
when I first had sex, it wasn't planned, and that she should think
about when and where she wanted her first sexual experience to
be, that she should be in control of her first sexual experience,
and she was. I did feel—I am not sure how I feel—maybe sad or
cheated—when she told me she was no longer a virgin, but I felt
good when she said she planned it, including having candles and
the right music. I felt I did good then.*

—Mama Opal

*I have tried to talk to my sons about sex a few times, but they
seem so uncomfortable. So I decided to just let them come to me
with questions, which they haven't. Presumably they are getting
enough information at school.*

—Mama Nico

*Sex has always been talked about. I think I am on overkill
because my fourteen-year-old often says that I am giving too
much info. I think I try to tell myself that she knows so much so it
won't kill me when I find out what she really does know. In
talking with her, though, I realize that she doesn't know a lot.
That is a problem, too. Acting without information. I told her
that sex is more interesting for women when you are old enough
to want to be pleasured as well as give pleasure to someone else.
If it's all about the other person, then you are not ready. This
discussion caused major eye rolling!*

—Mama Inga Aaron

And then I asked a group of teenagers, "What *should* parents tell their kids about sex?"

My little lesson on the birds and the bees happened on our way to pick up some bricks needed to complete a wall in the backyard. Cruising along Highway 205 in our red pickup, I learned all I needed to know and then some. I think that was smart. I was trapped and forced to listen.

—Mike, 16

Parents should tell their children exactly what sex is, and give good reasons why they wouldn't have sex at their child's age. Make sure you let them know that if they do choose to have sex, use condoms. If you have a girl, select a good method of birth control.

—Reese, 15

My mother told me straight up about the birds and the bees in detail when I asked where babies came from. I appreciated that a lot. She told me that I should try to wait until I'm married to have sex, but if I did it before then, "make sure you protect yourself." I lost my virginity at fourteen, but I took her advice on protecting myself.

—Jesse, 18

Sex . . . it's a word that comes to our minds a lot, but by the time kids are in junior high or high school, they already know everything—they don't need a "talk." If parents do talk to their children—maybe at ten years old—they should be straightforward and not confuse the child with animals or characters.

—NaeNae, 16

When I think about the conversations I have had with my parents, there is one topic that has never come up: sex. But I am proud to say that despite not having the "sex" conversation with my parents, I am eighteen years old and still a virgin.

—VaSheeta, 18

I strongly believe that when a child starts to emerge through puberty that it's your job as a parent to guide them through their sexual education. Would you rather your children's curiosity lead them into the hands of someone who doesn't care like you do—therefore giving invalid information? Sex is what brings new life, and also what can end lives. Is your child ready for either one of the results?

—"Hubba," 17

Personally, I think the sex talk is played out. No child actually finds out from their parents. They find out long before the parents even think of bringing it up. There is enough sex education at school to let us in on everything we need to know. All a sex talk with parents will do is make everyone feel awkward. Who seriously wants to hear their parents talk about sex?

—Alice, 17

LV + SX = LFE

The new teenager does *have sex earlier. The same
cultural changes that have given birth to the more
outspoken teenager have inaugurated a major change in
attitudes about sex. People talk about sex much more
openly. Sex between single men and women is not only
widely accepted but is done with a casualness that was
unthinkable not so many years ago. Teenagers are just
part of the trend: they have sex earlier, and more
casually as well.*

—Anthony E. Wolf, *Get Out of My Life, But First
Could You Drive Me and Cheryl to the Mall?*

*It was a decade of unbridled teenage sexual activity,
distinguished by the highest rate of adolescent
childbearing of the twentieth century. More than half of
all girls and boys lost their virginity while still in their
teens, and the number of illegitimate babies placed for*

adoption rose sharply. The decade? The 1950s.
—The American Academy of Pediatrics'
Caring for Your Teenager

Read a dozen reports on teenage sex and you'll get a dozen different stories. Which is it? When, exactly, was that chaste era "not so many years ago"? Were the '50s a decade of innocence and formality from which we've since descended into promiscuity? Or vice versa? Has adolescence always been a time of sexual experimentation? And what's really going on here and now?

I could ask my high school students, and I will. But how awkward is that?

I could tell you about the parts of my daughter's love life I am privy to—I've written about when I potty trained her and when she threw her biggest screaming-mad toddler fit—but when it comes to sexuality, I choose to leave her private life private.

We could look at the statistics. And we will. But sex statistics should always be taken with a grain of salt. People lie about sex, after all. Grownups lie about sex, and so do kids. The president of the United States lies about sex. People lie about masturbation and they lie about who they made out with last weekend. They lie about oral sex and they lie about intercourse. They lie about having it and they lie about not having it. Sex is, after all, taboo. And when it comes down to it, we don't know what's going on in anybody's bedroom but our own.

This country was founded on puritanical values that still permeate our law-making institutions from the White House to the local courthouses. Sexuality is advertised, sold, exploited, legislated, preached about, vilified, and hungered for. We associate sex with heaven, we associate sex with hell, and we associate sex with food. We associate sex with love, we associate sex with death, and we associate sex with the vastness of the universe. Young people are taught to be ashamed of sexual experience *and* inexperience. Teen sexuality is celebrated on sitcoms and in music videos on virtually every TV channel in America. And teen sex is illegal.

That sex is taboo drives it into the realm of secrets. That it's shrouded in secrecy gives rise to conflicting information. Conflicting information causes confusion. Confusion yields fear. And fear is the sole ingredient necessary to perpetuate a taboo.

Check this out:

Public Erections Outlawed

LOCUST, Penn., February 8, 2002—Councilors have unanimously passed a bill outlawing public erections and set a fine upwards of $300 for anyone appearing in public with an erect penis, even if said penis is covered by a pair of pants.

Although Locust reportedly had no history of problem public erections, town lawyer Todd Kerstetter said that "The supervisors are taking a proactive approach to protect the health, safety and morals of the community."

Sounds like a most unwelcoming place to come of age if you're a teenage boy!

Every culture, subculture, and generation has its own sexual norms. Depending on who you are and where you live, flaunting your sexuality can make you a star, or it can result in your being stoned to death.

A friend of mine told me about a teenager she knew who had a complete mental breakdown. Whenever someone suggested she get dressed, she screamed, "Why is everyone so afraid of my vagina?!"

Considering American attitudes about sexuality, her question doesn't seem all that crazy. The fact that *more* of our kids aren't any *more* confused about sex is a near-miraculous testament to human reason and basic sanity.

Researching crime statistics for this book, I routinely came across sexuality-related data thrown in with data about violence. Otherwise reasonable authors will note that "teen murder, suicide, and pregnancy rates are all on the rise." The fact that teen pregnancy is usually the result of consensual sex, and that it is neither violent nor intrinsically tragic doesn't seem to occur to these data-groupers. To be a murderer or to be a young mom is, apparently, equally offensive. In ads in *Teen People, Cosmo Girl!,* and other teen rags, the National Campaign to Prevent Teen Pregnancy uses sexy shots of waiflike adolescent boys and girls that one might just as soon expect to see in Calvin Klein commercials, but these ads are emblazoned with large, red labels like Reject, Dirty, Useless, Nobody, and Cheap. The minuscule print at the bottom of the page is only slightly less offensive. The ad featuring the "cheap" girl, for example, says, "Condoms are *cheap.* If we used one, I wouldn't have to tell my parents I'm pregnant."

"Well, maybe you would and maybe you wouldn't," Beth Lucht wrote in *Hip Mama* when the campaign was launched in 2000. "Condoms break and shit happens. Whether or not shit happens, having sex doesn't make a kid cheap."

I can't think of another class of Americans so openly ridiculed and insulted. Teen moms—and sexually active girls in general—take the heat in a society utterly confused about its own sexual values.

Regardless of what we did or did not do "forty years ago," most parents would rather our kids postpone becoming sexually active. We're not total hypocrites, but from a parent's point of view, sex is complicated. We don't want our kids to get a sexually transmitted disease. Frankly, most of us hope our kids will wait until they're finished with college to make us grandparents. But more than anything, we don't want our kids to get their hearts broken. And sex raises the stakes in a relationship. It's a matter of the body, but it's also a matter of the spirit and of the heart. So we have our preferences and we have our hopes, and we can express those freely to our kids, but we can also make sure our kids know we believe that their lives are their own. I've got rules for Maia, like the one that says she isn't allowed to solo date yet, but I also have basic respect—respect for privacy, choices, and individuality. I consider it part of my job to educate my daughter about safe sex and to let her know that sex isn't all about reproduction and disease, or all about intercourse.

Sex is lovely.

Sex is sacred.

Sex is serious.

Sex complicates things.

There is value in postponing sexual activity with another person.

And no matter what, sex doesn't make a kid dirty, useless, or cheap.

I consider it my job to be honest with my kid, but I don't necessarily consider it my job to know exactly what she's doing.

Our kids may or may not confide in us as they become sexually active, but I think if we're conscious, reasonable, and open, we can be a voice of sanity, even if that voice is just one of many.

Hopefully, by the time our kids are teenagers, we've already gotten somewhat used to our roles as sex educators. We've taught our kids the names for all their body parts and talked about puberty and development. We've been as honest as possible when discussing *every* realm of life, and in doing so built a rapport that doesn't place extra emphasis or anxiety on sex talk. The education simply *continues* through adolescence. But even if we've lagged a little in the early years, we can start now. Regardless of our values and opinions, I think all kids need sound information on anatomy, safe sex, birth control, and sexually transmitted diseases. Kids need to know that the rhythm method doesn't work and that condoms are the best protection against sexually transmitted diseases; they need to know where they can privately access birth control and teen health care if they need it. We're not going to get all of this across in a single "birds and bees" talk. Instead, we'll answer questions as they arise and broach the subject as we would any other topic on which there is a lot of misinformation floating around.

If you think you can just leave sex ed to your kid's school, here are some facts of life to ponder:
- Most teens say that they would prefer to get their information about pregnancy and birth control from their parents—but less than half of teens have had such a conversation.
- Parents and daughters communicate far more frequently than parents and sons on sexual facts, sociosexual issues, and morality.
- Three out of five teens say that they do not have enough information about how to use birth control, and almost half say

they don't know enough about where to get birth control.
- Five states prohibit or restrict the discussion of abortion in sex-ed classes. Eight states require or recommend that homosexuality be discussed as an unacceptable lifestyle and/or as a criminal offense under state law.
- Only twelve states, plus Washington, D.C., and Puerto Rico, require sex-ed teachers to be certified. In most states, sex ed is taught by teachers of other subjects, like home economics or physical education.
- Teens list television as one of their primary sources for information about sex. *Television!*
- Gay kids are still three times as likely as straight kids to attempt suicide.

In addition to providing our kids with information and resources, we can educate ourselves about the sexual norms in the country and in our communities. This is the larger world in which our kids are coming of age, and it's going to have an impact on their choices and experiences. Statistics are disputable, but I think they do give us insight into the cultural expectations that are the backdrop to our kids' sexual unfurling.

If you're in high school and you've never gotten any—whether you don't want to or just can't—you can stop worrying: You are now officially the statistical norm.

—Rolling Stone

According to the American Academy of Pediatrics, the average age of first intercourse is sixteen. Between 1983 and 1999, the percentage of high school students with sexual experience fell from 59 to 50%. And according to the Centers for Disease Control and Prevention, condom use among teenagers rose from 11% in 1983 to 58% in 1999. In other words, there's a pretty good chance that our kids will actually be *less* promiscuous and *less* likely to take sexual risks than we were.

In *Millennials Rising,* Howe and Strauss write that this counterrevolution has something to do with the success of sex ed, something to do with the conservative "chastity movement," and an awful lot to do with the fact that instead of seeing their parents as a bunch of hung-up, repressed old farts, our kids tend to see us as pleasure driven and sex obsessed.

I was once on a sex-ed panel with Susie "Sexpert" Bright. Noting that many of her own sexual fantasies came out of the taboos of her Catholic upbringing, she joked, "What's my daughter going to fantasize about? Sunset walks on the beach?"

If the new reports reflect reality, she probably will.

But do they reflect reality? I interviewed a number of eighteen- to twenty-one-year-olds to try and find out. Interestingly, all of their claims about their own lives suggested that the stats are right-on, but many of them had explanations for why they were such "late bloomers." They told me, "I went to an all-girls school," or "I didn't live in the city," or "I *did* live in the city, so my parents never let me out of their sight," or "I was just a geek." So while kids—like their parents—are under the impression that "everybody's doing it," the bottom line is that about half of all kids graduate from high school virgins.

It's important to keep these facts—or possibilities—in mind when we're talking to our kids about sex. When I was a teenager, friends of my parents assumed I was sexually active long before I was. Afraid of being judged a "prude," and also to reclaim my privacy, I gave my parents the impression that I'd lost my virginity about a year before I actually had. Looking back, it seems fairly silly. But it didn't *feel* silly at the time. So it's important not to make assumptions. For all you know, your kid took a secret virginity pledge at twelve, is holding out for his wedding night, and will be completely offended if you assume that he's having sex with his girlfriend.

That in mind, it's also important for us, as parents, to be clear about our own opinions. Teen sex isn't a value-free topic, after all. If we disapprove of premarital sex, we can be open about that. If we disapprove of repression, we can impart that without embarrassing our kids. If we have religious beliefs that influence our attitudes, we can explain those. If we feel hung up or nervous talking about sex, we can acknowledge that. Our kids deserve to know who we are and where we stand. They may or may not agree with us, and they may or may not adopt our values, but being clear with ourselves and with our kids provides a structure and a grounding from which they can make their own decisions. If our expectations of our children are too extreme, we might get lied to. But we can do our best to lay out our own ethics and, at the same time, communicate our love. And we can assure them that we won't reject them if they make choices that go against our preferences.

You Feel Weird above Your Stomach When You See Them

I asked fifteen- and sixteen-year-olds, "What is love?"

Ignorance
Happiness
A word I can manipulate
Two people
You can't live without it
Mysterious
Amazing
Caring about someone else
    more than yourself
Delightful
Silly
The greatest high in the world
Every emotion
A summer evening
Loyalty

Feeling so passionate about someone
  you can't live without them
Complete acceptance
An unbreakable bond of affection
Something that everyone wants but
  some won't get
Hard to find
Stupid
Caring for someone regardless of
  what happens
An illusion
A chemical reaction
You feel weird above your stomach
  when you see them
Can't be apart for a second
You must spend your life with that
  person
Indescribable
Unknown (What *is* known is bullshit)
The feeling that gravity is lost
How can you tell lust from love? Or
  even peer pressure from love?
Pain
The feeling that there's no one else
  in the world
Understanding
Something
I give up
How the fuck am I supposed to know?

"Why I Have No Resentment"

Over the summer, I had the pleasure of meeting Gabrielle, a twenty-year-old college student from the Bronx. "Now there's a nice young lady," I thought to myself.

We were sitting at my friend Inga's kitchen table, drinking coffee.

Gabby was in town doing an internship as Inga's research assistant.

Superintelligent and ambitious, silly and sociable, she had the air of someone who'd managed to get smart without getting her spirit crushed. And I like that in a girl. When I found out how young she was, I couldn't help but wonder if she was just born well-adjusted or if her parents had a little something to do with it. The morning before she left town in late August, I asked her to get up early and enlighten me.

Me: How would you describe your upbringing?
Gabrielle: I had the strictest parents in the whole world. Up until I was thirteen, we went to bed at 8:30 P.M. No questions. They checked the homework, and if there was something wrong with it, you had to do it over again.

I didn't have curfews because they dropped me off and picked me up everywhere I went. They knew all my friends' parents. It was like that until I was seventeen.

In high school, they kind of mellowed out, and now with my younger brother—he can go wherever he wants.

Me: So your parents were a lot stricter than your friends' parents?
Gabrielle: Yeah. My homegirl, Anna, her mother was an alcoholic. A lovable alcoholic, but an alcoholic nonetheless. So Anna could basically do what she wanted from a very young age. It wasn't totally reckless, but it was reckless. She would come to my house and fall in love with my parents because they were present. And I would go over to her house and fall in love with her mother because she would let me do whatever I wanted. Most of my friends didn't have two parents in the house, so they loved coming over to my house. They called us the Puerto Rican Brady Bunch.

Me: Looking back, do you feel your parents were too strict?
Gabrielle: Not at all.

Now, my dad used to be heavy-handed with us. They were strict. I hated it.

And at one point my mom freaked out on me. My last year of high school we didn't really get along. We never really talked about it, but I think it was her time of realizing "my baby's going to college," and she didn't know how to deal with it.

One time I came home from school and she started yelling at me about the dishes. I was doing everything at school. I was the student body president and everything. I said, "Why are you yelling at me? I just got home."

And she said, "Well, no one asked you to come home."

I couldn't believe it. My mother had never said anything like that to me. I just started bawling.

Their strictness had a lot to do with the church influence, but it also had to do with a fear of the neighborhood. Both my parents had grown up in the Bronx, and they watched the news, so they were just afraid. But I have no resentment toward them. They did what they thought was best. And they just had a hard time letting go.

Minus the scarier aspects of my upbringing—minus the hitting, minus the religion—I would totally advocate strictness. They didn't shelter us. They told us what was going on. They told us *why* we couldn't do things. A lot of my friends felt that their parents didn't care about them. I had a really safe home to come to.

Me: How about your romantic life?

Gabrielle: I was not allowed to have a boyfriend. Boys were bad news. "Dirty girls" had boyfriends. I had this best friend named Leo. We were cuddling on the couch one day. My mom pulled me aside and said, "That is a no-no!" So I wasn't allowed to have a boyfriend.

They said homosexuals were an "abomination in the eyes of Christ." It was a "sin against God," which always bummed me out even before I had any inclination of my own queerness.

One time I had a conversation with my dad about it. I said, "How can you say they're going to hell? Your own brother is gay."

And he said, "Well, everyone has their own personal relationship with God, so no one can know for sure where someone else is going. Maybe if they have a close personal relationship with God, they will be forgiven."

So I thought, *all right.*

Me: Did you follow your parents' rules, or did you sneak around?
Gabrielle: Oh, I knew where the boys were. When I hung out with Anna, we met the boys. They were at the train station. My first kiss was at a train station.

Me: How old were you?
Gabrielle: Fifteen. Then I started going to this art center, and I fell in love with this boy named Derick. I was afraid to get physical with boys, though. I thought I would get pregnant or get a disease. That was from Catholic school, too. At Catholic school, they told us that condoms didn't work, that even condoms with spermicide didn't work. They told us that if we had sex and we used a condom with spermicide, a sperm could get through anyway and then we would have these green babies.

Me: So where did you get your sex education?
Gabrielle: MTV.

Me: MTV?
Gabrielle: Yeah, MTV. The first time I ever saw two boys kiss was on MTV. I got real information on safe sex. And the Internet. I found out how to have sex, what an orgasm was. I talked to girls on the Internet. That's how I started to explore my interest in girls. So, I had girlfriends online and boyfriends in real life.

Me: How was it at school—was your high school homophobic?
Gabrielle: Catholic school was the most aggressively homophobic place I have ever encountered. My friends. And myself. One time there was a new girl at my school. It came out that she had kissed a girl in

the past, and people tortured her and screamed "dyke!" in her face and wrote "lesbo" on her locker. I never said anything to her, but I never said anything *for* her, either.

It was a hard place to be confused about myself. At one point someone thought I was a lesbian, and she said, "I don't think I can be friends with you anymore." They were having sex with their boyfriends, but when it came to homosexuality, suddenly it was a religious issue.

Me: So you didn't come out until you were in college?

Gabrielle: I actually ended up telling one person in high school I thought I was gay. And there was this woman before I got to college. But I was totally in love with Derick. When I went to college, all the gayest men fell in love with me. Then, my first birthday at school, someone had a party for me. I was drunk. And in walks the most beautiful girl. It was like *West Side Story*. I spent the rest of the night telling her, "I'm not gay, but you're the most beautiful girl I've ever seen in my life." We fell in love, and she was my girlfriend for two and a half years. I never had a problem at school. Everybody loved us.

I ended up telling my aunt. She was the most heterosexual cop—but she had always given me a place to stay when I was having trouble with my parents. I was at her house and she was, like, "Are there any boys?"

And I was like, "Well . . ."

And she was like, "More than one boy?!"

And I was like, "Well, actually, it's a girl."

She was like, "Get me a drink!"

I went to the kitchen and I got her a margarita and we talked about it.

A year later, I told my brother. He was freaked out. He was weird for about a week, but then he was fine.

Another year later, I decided to tell my parents. I was scared because I knew what they had said. I knew. I didn't think I'd have a mother anymore. And I just love my mother. But finally I couldn't lie anymore. I was with my girlfriend and sneaking around. I was like, OK, my homegirl Anna has been on her own since she was sixteen years old. Even if I won't have a mother anymore, I can do this. I decided to tell them after Christmas. I thought, *Let's enjoy Christmas.* I had my aunt ready to come pick me up. I had another friend on call. My brother knew I was planning to tell them. He was shitting bricks. I was sitting at the table. I was crying. I said, "I have something to tell you."

My mom said, "It's OK if you're pregnant."

I said, "I'm not pregnant. But this February 14 is my two-year anniversary with my girlfriend."

My mom just got really red in the face and didn't say anything.

I said, "I've made my peace with God."

My dad was saying, "We love you no matter what," but then when he realized my mother wasn't saying anything, he stopped saying "we" and he started saying "I."

I said, "Do I still have a place to stay?" Because I was sure I wouldn't have a place to live and I wouldn't be able to go back to college.

My mom stood up. I thought she was going to walk away, but she walked around the table to me and she just broke down and put her arms around me and said, "Of course you have a place to stay. I love you."

It was weird for a while after that. My mother said, "Did I do anything?" and "Who made you this way?" It baffles my mom, which is really kind of cute. She said, "Were you just really good friends first?"

I said, "No. It was exactly the same as it was with Derick. She walked in and I just had this feeling. It's exactly the same."

The other day, she said, "When you have babies . . . or when you get inseminated . . ." And I was like, *Oh my god! My mom said "inseminated"!*

But I was just so shocked that I could still be at home and could still go to school. I just thanked God. That's why I have no resentment towards my parents. They are beautiful people who just grow with me and just love me. Thank God.

Things That Keep Us Up at Night

Sometimes this broken heart gives birth to anxiety and panic, sometimes to anger, resentment, and blame. But under the hardness of that armor there is the tenderness of genuine sadness. This is our link with all those who have ever loved. This genuine heart of sadness can teach us great compassion. It can humble us when we're arrogant and soften us when we are unkind. It awakens us when we prefer to sleep and pierces through our indifference.

—Pema Chödrön, *The Places That Scare You*

Waiting Up

How handy is this? The American Academy of Pediatrics' guidelines for setting curfews:

Age	12–13	14–16	17–21
School nights	7 P.M.–8 P.M.	8 P.M.–9 P.M.	10 P.M.–11 P.M.
Weekends	9 P.M.–10 P.M.	10 P.M.–11 P.M.	12 A.M.–1 A.M.
Special-event nights	Negotiable, but no later than midnight	Negotiable, but no later than midnight	Negotiable, but no later than 2 A.M.

Waiting up: mostly it's boring. I'm tired. A summer night. The fan cooling the sweltering air just slightly. I'm not worried—not yet—but the what-ifs do dance across my mind every fifteen or twenty minutes. A familiar, free-floating anxiety that reminds me of her first afternoons at daycare, her first mornings in kindergarten, the nights she used to visit her dad. What if someone broke into the house where she's baby-sitting? What if she forgot to turn off the stove after making one of the kids a tofu dog? What if the mothers came home drunk and, too embarrassed to call me, attempted to drive her?

It's getting late. She should be here soon. I'm yawning sleepy, but there's no question: I will stay up.

I double-check that the phone is plugged in, the ringer on. The line needs to be open for the call I hope will not come. No news is good news. Unless she's very late, in which case no news could be good news or bad news.

The grandmother clock strikes its midnight bells, one after another, reverberating through the living room and hallway, but the grandmother clock runs five or ten minutes fast. She should be home any minute. I fidget and yawn, file my nails.

She's baby-sitting for a few young mamas down the street while they're off at the Snoop Dogg show. Anything could be holding them up, and in turn, holding her up.

To call at this point would be silly.

Instead, I flip on the TV. The entertainment channel has a segment called "It's Good to Be Michael Jackson." I do not think it would be good to be Michael Jackson. On the women's channel, it's *Unsolved Mysteries*. Don't you hate the way the host of that show says "*UN-soooolved MYS-teries*"? I turn off the tube. *Unsolved Mysteries* is the last thing I need. It's such a scam that "television for women" is all paranoia-feeding slit throats and kidnappings, unrelenting stalkers and women scorned. Programming for men is full of fart jokes and football, politics and sexy beach babes. Do men really have nothing to worry about?

A car screeches around a corner a few blocks away. It's 12:20 A.M. now and I'm going to call even though I might wake up three sleeping babes.

Maia knows perfectly well to call me if she's running late. And I told the mamas midnight. Midnight does not mean 12:20 A.M. I smile, think it's funny that now I'm getting parental on the young moms as well as on my kid. Then I remember to be pissed off. Giggles and anger are both so much more comfortable than fear.

One of the moms answers the phone, sounds as tired as I am. "They're not back yet?" she says, sounding alarmed. "They left quite a while ago."

The house is four blocks from ours. What does "quite a while ago" mean? I'm not laughing now. I'm trying to stay mad so the fear won't settle. "Then, where are they?" I snap.

"Well," she hums, "they might have stopped at the bank . . ."

Just then I hear the car out front. Footsteps on the porch. It's too soon to be the cops, so I know it's my girl-child.

"It was hard," she says as she steps inside. "The kids are cute, but they wouldn't go to sleep. And the clock stopped at nine P.M., and I just kept glancing at it and I didn't realize it had totally stopped. I thought time was just standing still. I meant to put the kids to bed before midnight. But I thought it was nine. Then the moms didn't have any money. We had to go to the bank. What time is it? I'm sorry."

"I was worried," I admit. "But it sounds like you did a good job."

It's hardly worth scolding her over, let alone punishing her. I don't need to go off on her just because I got nervous. But this is an issue I had no guidance for as a parent. I can be pretty clueless when it comes to structure. I can't remember ever having a curfew as a kid, and everyone I talk to has such different standards—and different boiling points. With a curfew, I know when to start seriously bugging out. And with the help of a working timepiece, Maia can know exactly when I'll be bugging, too. Here's where the American Academy of Pediatrics comes in. *Caring for Your Teenager: The Complete and Authoritative Guide* is such a dorky-looking thing—thicker than the Bible and designed like your middle school Spanish textbook—I never would have picked it up had I not been researching *this* book, but I highly recommend it. It offers some of the most reasonable, down-to-earth advice I've found. Granted, some of the information I'll never use, and the academy's worldview is obviously pro–Western medicine. Still, sometimes it's incredibly handy to know what "normal" people do. If we don't want to do the same, that's cool. But it gives us a reference point. There's nothing I'm willing to do about the fact that Maia wants me to dress "normal." But now she can have a curfew just like the Huxtables.

Her baby-sitting job counted as a "special-events night," so my little chart gave me the "no later than midnight" guideline. In trying to figure out a curfew, we can factor in our kid's level of responsibility, his or her opinion on the matter, the laws in our community, and our own priorities, but the chart offers a starting place.

So what *consequences* make sense when kids stay out too late? Except in the event of something unforeseen—like a stopped clock and cashless baby-sitting clients—the AAP recommends simply deducting time from future curfews. An hour late and they lose an hour next Friday night. Two hours late and maybe they can *forget* next Friday night. Longer-term punishments—like grounding the kid for a month—amount to overkill. But having *no* consequences would make the curfew a joke. Whatever standards you want to develop are fine, but I think it's important to figure out those standards before you're up late watching *UN-sooolved MYS-teries* and freaking out about where the hell your baby is. Getting scared is natural, but turning into Paranoid Rage Mama is usually unnecessary, and hella unfun.

Who's on Drugs?

As the parent of a teenager, *you* are at least as likely to be on drugs as your kid.

Yep. Most drinking, smoking, pill-popping waste cases are grownups, not teens. According to the American Academy of Pediatrics, about one in ten teenagers uses drugs. About one in six, however, has a parent who uses. But that's *our* problem, right? And *do as I say, kids, not as I do.*

Conventional wisdom holds that one of the big, bad realities of raising teens is that they'll start abusing drugs. "Peer pressure" is supposed to be the monster. Because drugs were such an intrinsic part of American youth culture when we came of age in the '60s, '70s, and '80s, we have plenty of memories to back up our concerns. And while youth drug culture is not a thing of the past, baby boomers—followed by Gen Xers—remain the major consumers of illegal drugs. A 2003 national survey of high school students found that fewer than 10% felt pressured to use.

At a recent Thanksgiving dinner, I found myself baby-sitting a toddler while his mother was in the backyard smoking a joint—hiding from both him and her own parents. *Her* parents were on the front porch, also smoking a joint—hiding from both their daughter and grandson. When these stoners start telling the boy to "just say no," it's going to be pretty hard for them not to sound like hypocrites.

In addition to illegal drugs, prescription drugs have become a fact of life for American adults, and a generation of youngsters.

Ritalin—a patented and legal version of speed—is prescribed to millions of children every year. Controversial and highly addictive, Ritalin has been linked to drug-abuse problems later in life. Still, its use is widespread, even for the very young. Ritalin prescriptions to children between the ages of two and four doubled in the early 1990s. Soon to follow was an increase in antidepressant use. According to Food and Drug Administration data, prescriptions of antidepressants to preschoolers increased tenfold in the mid–'90s. In 1994 alone, three thousand Prozac prescriptions were written for children who had yet to reach their first birthday.

Three thousand babies got prescriptions for Prozac.

As our kids enter their teen years, many of them have been on drugs all of their lives. And they've gotten those drugs from *us*.

In early 2003, a new drug hyped in national TV and magazine ads began offering parents an alternative to Ritalin for treating attention deficit disorder. The ads promise an "ordinary" life to families who give their kids Strattera, a "non-stimulant medication for ADHD [attention deficit hyperactivity disorder]." Sounds like some kind of decaf Ritalin, but Strattera is actually a selective norepinephrine reuptake inhibitor similar to drugs used for depression and panic. Parents have already started reporting that, in addition to the company's listed side effects, which range from appetite loss to mood swings, the drug can inspire anger, bouts of violence, obsession with death, nightmares, and hallucinations. As the Strattera ads say, "Welcome to ordinary."

Ordinary, indeed.

Hundreds of thousands of teens take antidepressants regularly— "legitimately" as well as recreationally. A 1999 study by the University of North Carolina at Chapel Hill found that 72% of physicians acknowledged having prescribed antidepressants to patients under eighteen, even though only 8% of those doctors said they had received adequate training in the management of childhood depression.

If it's a teenage wasteland out there, we've got no one but ourselves to blame. We are teaching our kids that if they have a problem, we have a pill for it.

In the summer of 2003, warnings by drug regulators about the safety of Paxil—one of the most widely prescribed antidepressants— reopened questions about a whole class of drugs that also includes Prozac and Zoloft. Reports from British doctors endorsed by the FDA showed that Paxil carried a substantial risk of prompting teenagers and children to consider suicide. Because the studies also showed that Paxil was no more effective than placebos in treating young people's depression, regulators recommended that doctors write no new Paxil prescriptions for patients under eighteen.

Much has been made of the fact that Eric Harris, one of the Columbine High School killers, was on Luvox—a selective serotonin reuptake inhibitor like Paxil, Prozac, and Zoloft. The insert for Luvox listed mania, apathy, and psychosis as *frequent* adverse reactions. Other school shooters known to have been on antidepressants at the time of their attacks include fifteen-year-old Kip Kinkel, who, while on Prozac, killed his parents and then traveled to school, where he opened fire on classmates, killing two and wounding twenty-two others; fourteen-year-old Elizabeth Bush, on antidepressants when she wounded one student at her Pennsylvania high school; and eighteen-year-old Jason Hoffman, on Effexor and Celexa when he wounded one teacher and three students at his California high school.

These are potentially dangerous drugs, and our kids are getting them from *us*. The pro–prescription drug folks claim that antidepressants have prevented more suicides and murders than they've caused, but there is no evidence to back up that claim. The truth about all these new drugs is that we simply do not know.

Cocaine, marijuana, and LSD have, frankly, been around a lot longer than any of these antidepressants. We know what they do. We know the dangers. But if you wouldn't have wanted your kids to take part in an electric Kool-Aid acid test, you ought to think long and hard before agreeing with some doctor about what chemical your kid needs to feel better—particularly if this doctor hasn't had adequate training in the *non*chemical treatment of adolescent emotional problems.

Three thousand babies got prescriptions for Prozac.

Were those little beings—who couldn't even walk or talk yet—going to kill themselves or someone else? I don't think so.

Three thousand babies got prescriptions for Prozac. Those babies are going to be teenagers soon. And when we start telling them to "just say no," it's going to be pretty hard not to sound like hypocrites.

One February 14, I received a call from Maia's elementary school teacher, who informed me that my daughter had had a panic attack while opening her valentines. The teacher then suggested that I get my child on anti-anxiety medication. This proposal, in my view, was obscene. That this same teacher would have been obliged to expel Maia had she found her with a bag of weed only proves that we are living in a crazy-ass world. Am I saying that I want my daughter to smoke weed? No. I want my daughter to learn to handle her emotions. And the way one learns to handle one's emotions is by experiencing them.

Now, I'm elated that mental illness has been stripped of some of its social stigma in recent years. Truly, I am. Psychiatric intervention and, in some cases, psychopharms can be a godsend for deeply disturbed people who can't otherwise function as they wish to. Some teenagers, like those suffering from bipolar disorder and severe depression that cannot be remedied by other life changes or family therapy, may benefit from mood stabilizers. But psychopharms are *not* for every baby who looks bummed, or every elementary school kid who's anxious about her valentines, or every teenager who might have been perfectly content with a copy of *The Teenage Liberation Handbook* and permission to drop out of school.

In times of war, stolen elections, environmental degradation, and economic exploitation, sensitive people have a hard time. This is not because there is something wrong with their brain chemistries. For people who can hear the earth crying, sadness is inevitable. It is a valid emotion. Should we all feel good in bad situations? Would the civil rights movement ever have happened if those generations of activists had had antidepressants at their fingertips? Sometimes depression is an energy-draining, ambition-zapping dead end. But sometimes the unendurable is the beginning of a glorious arc of activism. Antidepressants blunt our sadness, but they also blunt our joy. And sometimes our problems are not in our heads.

If our kids are considering—or are already regularly using—legal or illegal drugs, it might be time for us to help them rethink their lives.

Are they depressed? Why? What are their options for remedying that depression? The solutions might be simple or drastic—but all solutions are *possible*. What do our kids suggest?

Dietary changes, turning off the TV, activism, homeopathy, acupuncture, and counseling are all low-risk interventions. If none of those have a noticeable impact, what else can we do?

Are our kids looking for a bonding experience with friends? Are they in need of an initiation into what they see as the adult world? How can we help them achieve these goals in a relatively safe way?

Maybe school sucks. How can we help make it better? It's never too late to start homeschooling or unschooling. American high schools are not for everyone. And the truly beautiful thing about the American educational system is that anyone can drop out, take the GED, enter a private or community college at a later date, and go on to a higher education when and if the time is right. I dropped out of my drug-infested high school at the beginning of my junior year, took three years off to travel and have a baby, and returned to complete an undergrad and graduate education just one year "behind" my traditional-track peers.

Are our kids hating us or the communities we live in? Why? What are their options? Can we change something? Can they go and live with another relative? Can they go and build latrines in the developing world? They *can*. Our kids need to know that wholly other lives can be arranged.

I do not own a home and do not have a college-savings account, but I put away fully 10% of *whatever* my income is every month to be sure that other lives can be arranged.

This is not about sending our kids off to boarding school the first time we catch them drinking a beer or smoking weed. Some drug and alcohol use for some kids is age appropriate and not indicative of any deeper issues. But even if our kids are "just experimenting" with non-life-threatening substances, they need to know that this is not the 1970s. The country they live in is approaching a police state. Getting busted for drugs can mean going to jail, and we may not be able to bail them out immediately. Our kids need to consider what they want, and the risks they're willing to take. Sadly, a fourteen-year-old sparking up a joint is probably not able to make an informed decision about those risks. But as parents, we need to be and stay real with our kids. We need to talk to our kids about the reality of drug use, the reality of the law, and the reality of the other life options open to them. And if we don't want our kids to get hooked on addictive substances, we need to quit ourselves. If we honestly can't quit, then we need to be real about that, too. Our failed attempts at getting sober may serve as real examples of human addiction our kids will want to avoid.

The line between reality and reality TV blurs, and we are the f***ing Osbournes. As Ozzy says, "I'm not proud of being a drug addict and alcoholic. I'm not proud of biting the head off a bat or biting the head off a dove. But it could be worse—I could be Sting."

Welcome to ordinary.

Do Not Feel Like a Freak

I asked the parents of teenagers, "What has been the hardest thing about this job?"

I thought I would be free now. But they eat so much, and they want me to buy them so much. It's a heavy weight, to care for them and shoulder their anger.

—Mama Kara

Making sure my daughter, who struggled with dyslexia, got the best education available. She went to an experimental school, then a school for dyslexic kids, then made it through senior year at the local public school with a C average. I felt good about that. Oh . . . she also got expelled for a week for being caught smoking dope. I was more worried, however, about the constant pressure from a few of the girls to get her to go into prostitution. . . . I was worried that the money they offered her would sway her into doing something stupid. I increased her allowance.

—Mama Lynn

The kids came to live with me when they were thirteen and sixteen. I know this broke their mother's heart, but I expected to be able to set some boundaries with them and give them things she couldn't. Instead I just feel like she got the glory years of parenting while I get the hardship. My sons lie to me. They sneak out. I worry about them because I love them deeply, but I also— selfishly, I know—feel that I cannot fail. What if something happens to them on my watch?

—Papa Daniel

The hardest thing I have done, by far, was to make the decision to send my daughter to a treatment center for her mental illness. I had to risk that she would hate me forever in order to take a chance that she could get well. When your child is little and gets a scrape, you wash it out and you sing and entertain them while you do it, and tell them that it will only hurt for a minute and it does only hurt for a minute, and they smile when it is over and run right back outside to play some more. Sending my girl to live in another place was not going to be over in a minute. Would she ever forgive me? I had no idea. (She has. In fact, she is glad now that she is there and getting well, steadily.)

—Mama Alice

Despite all the constant battling and emotional frenzy, the absolute hardest, gut-wrenching thing has been to let him go and live with his dad for a while. I'm in New Hampshire and his dad is in Georgia. I've never been apart from him for more than a weekend before, let alone a thousand miles distant. You dread the day they may ask to go live with the other parent . . . especially when you feel the atmosphere at the other parent's home, while not dangerous or abusive, is far, far from your acceptable levels of parenting . . . where everything is the opposite of what you care about/worry about/hope for/avoid/believe in/defend/ despise/try to teach your child. . . . It's a living nightmare. You know that it is the right thing to do; you know that it is a journey that he needs to take to find himself, to rid himself of illusions and crutches that are only hindering and limiting his potential; you know that it is the Right Action to take, but you still can't help but take it personally. It feels like a car slamming into you at full speed, smashing the breath right out of you, and you live in a suspended state of asphyxiation. . . . You grieve for them when you pass their room at the top of the stairs, when you set the table and that place is empty, when you see something that they would like, or laugh at. . . . You worry and worry and hope that nothing terrible happens because you are terrified of how the other parent might screw it up. . . . You lie awake at night with your obsessions roiling through your mind about all the things that could go wrong, that they won't come back, and worst of all that they may absorb and exhibit those tendencies and personality traits of their other parent that are your deepest fears. . . . The hardest thing is having to step back, be strong, and let them do this, when it rips your heart out but you know it is the right choice to help them grow.

—Mama Suess

My daughter keeps finding ways to harm herself. I think she has now done every single thing mentioned in the book Reviving Ophelia. *At age fourteen she was suicidal. She had a friend who really was bulimic, suicidal, and manic-depressive. She got overly caught up in this friend's troubles. That, along with other angst and the teen hormones, threw my daughter over the edge. I'm worried about her constantly. What is she doing? What will she do next? Where is she? What does she have hiding in her bedroom? When I was pregnant with her, I agonized over taking even one aspirin. I had natural childbirth at home. I breast-fed her for five years. She never had baby formula. When she was sick as a child, I almost always treated her with homeopathy. As a teen, she has been on antidepressants. Now she smokes pot and drinks. She has cut herself. She was suicidal and took a lot of aspirin one time, but fortunately threw up. She is currently borderline anorexic and most recently has made herself throw up. We are in therapy for these things. She is actually fairly happy these days, doing well in school and being responsible in most ways, but keeps finding strange, harmful ways to deal with her overall anxiety.*

—Mama Kathy

Do not feel like a freak if you think this is hard. I thought babies were incredibly hard. Just so hard. Well, this is harder. My oldest is a real workout. She will be sixteen next week. We have had some big growing pains. Partying, boys, smoking, shoplifting, wild angry tantrums. Thank Maude she does fairly well in school, but even that has had some hits. She dropped her sport. It has been so difficult. I could tell you stuff that would make your kid seem like a total angel.

—Mama Mariah

Brood

Summertime: I'm feeling like Maia has all but moved out. After four nights of slumber-party-hopping she's finally back, but she just mopes around the house like being home is a prison sentence.

I say, "What's going on with you?"

She says, "Nothing."

I say, "You seem pissed off."

She says, "No."

I say, "Or sad."

She says, "No."

And so I drop it. She's free to feel how she feels, after all; free to talk about it or not talk about it. But her depression, when it settles, envelops everything around her, my heart included. Dark cloud of sad, pissed-off doom.

"Let teenagers brood," my friend Caprice says. "Back in the day, when the kids all worked on the family farm, there was no time for all of this *talking about feelings*. Let it go."

And so I let it go. It will pass. Or it won't.

I want to accept the inevitable estrangement that comes along with growing up. I want to let her individuate from me. I want to allow space for her moods. But I miss knowing her well. I miss the open weeping that used to accompany her sad days. I miss the speed with which her depression used to pass. I miss being her confidante. I miss the ease with which she used to forgive me my flaws.

I fear I won't know the difference between healthy silences and dangerous silences. As mama and kid, we were close. Now I wonder if we were too close. Would this separation be easier if I hadn't tried my hand at attachment parenting? Quiet, quiet. She is too much like me.

The years stretch out in front of us. We are only just now on the brink of it all. What if I don't have it in me? Why is this so hard for me? She isn't even defiant. She just wants to brood. I long for an outburst.

I Completely Shut Down

I asked a group of teenagers, "What has made communication difficult in your family?"

I never have difficulty approaching my parents—they are open-minded and willing to take time out to listen to me—but not always will I tell them everything. It's not like I did something wrong and I don't want them to find out, it's just little things that I can handle on my own and not get them worried about.

—Toan, 17

I always want to discuss things with my parents, but about many things I receive that "don't bother me" expression. They love me, but they just don't know how to talk to me. We are different people from different generations, born and raised differently. They're from Laos, things were harder there. I'm a U.S. child, I'm more rebellious and stand on stronger ground.

—Nahna, 17

My parents actually know me well, but sometimes there are things I just don't want them to know. Just like there are things they don't want to know—I call it healthy neglect.

—Cody, 16

For the last three months, my caregiver and I haven't been talking to each other at all because of something very stupid. She feels that everything I do is bad, so she will not talk to me. I feel that if she is not going to talk to me, then I have no desire to talk to her. My whole family has lack of communication. It's as if my feelings just don't matter to anyone. I really feel that she thinks the world revolves around her. To make this family work, everyone needs to grow up.

—Joshua, 16

My sister drowned a couple of years ago. She was the closest to me and when I lost her I completely shut down. I didn't want to talk or think about what happened. I was in complete denial. My parents couldn't help me because they were going through the same thing. For a while things were disoriented, but eventually I was able to talk about her death. It just took a lot of time and comfort from family and friends.

—Gloria, 15

My parents and I don't have good communication. We don't talk about our feelings or what's on our minds. They just tell me the dos and don'ts and I'm supposed to follow. I pretty much only talk to them when I need or want something. I, personally, like it like this. It's probably because I'm used to it.

If the communication between my parents and I grew, it'd be kind of weird and awkward.

—Tien, 17

It took a while for me to open up to my mother because of her intimidating personality. She's the type of person you'd be scared to approach because of the way her voice carries and her way of thinking. Opening up to her and telling her things I'd only discuss with a close friend was difficult because I feared her reaction. I decided, though, that if the things I was doing couldn't be talked about, I shouldn't be doing them. If I was going to make grown-up decisions, I shouldn't be afraid to share them with my mother.

—Princess, 18

Is Talking Overrated?

*The most heartbreaking thing for me was that my sweet,
loving, expressive son suddenly became very private and
short on words. Virtually every question was answered
with "yeah," "naw," "nothing," or a shrug. I thought he'd
fallen into some kind of a depression, but he still seemed
to enjoy his friends, and he still joked and laughed
about some things with me. It's just that the deep
conversations became few and far between. I wanted in
on his emotional world, and there was just this huge
Keep Out sign.*

—Mama June

Silence makes us nervous.

It's scary because it's hard to know what's going on with people—with our kids—when they don't *tell* us. But talking isn't always the key to happiness.

Silence, repression, and stoicism all got bad names in the twentieth century. Therapy culture taught us to express ourselves, to talk about our issues. If we were abuse survivors, for example, part of therapy culture encouraged us to introduce ourselves—and keep on introducing ourselves—with our wounds: "Hi, my name is Ariel, and I'm an abuse survivor." We broke our silences. But then many of us got stuck there. I mean, what's wrong with "Hi, my name is Ariel, and I'm the author of four books"? Or "Hi, my name is Ariel, and I'm a kick-ass child of the universe"? What's wrong with not leading with our brokenness?

Therapy culture gave us an emotional language. But an emotional language is not a cure-all. Prior to the advent of psychiatry and pop psychology, we had poetry. And the poets have always known that while language can heal, silence can heal, too.

The word "repression" conjures up images of anal-retentive grumps and hysterical amnesiacs, but in experimental psychology, "repression" just means coping with problems by minimizing, distracting, or denying them. And new research suggests that those of us who use these repressive techniques can deal with the ups and downs of our lives just as well—if not better—than the ramblers.

"Stoicism," for its part, is described in my American Heritage dictionary as "indifference to pain or pleasure." The dreaded teenage apathy and the heartless stone. But Stoicism is actually an ancient Hellenistic philosophy that taught disciples (many of them teenagers) how to achieve inner calm in the midst of a chaotic world. Stoics believed that to avoid unhappiness, frustration, and disappointment, they needed to learn to control those things within their power (their own beliefs, attitudes, and desires) and develop indifference to those things *not* within their power. It isn't exactly an activist philosophy, but we all might take a clue from the Stoics—and from our seemingly apathetic teens—when it comes to not stressing out over things we can't control.

The question of when it's considered all right to express ourselves and when society would rather we put up and shut up is a gendered issue. Our girls learn to articulate their emotional lives freely, but to repress direct aggression. Our boys, on the other hand, are allowed—encouraged—to express their aggression, but are still expected "take it like a man" when it comes to their vulnerabilities. They learn to repress their love, their fears, and their self-doubt.

Recent revolutions in our thinking about raising sons have helped us embolden our boys to develop their emotional selves. "Girl power" and feminist movements have heartened us to make room for female aggression. These changes represent major progress. Removing sexism from the equation is vital. But neither the traditionally male "suck it up and punch someone" nor the traditionally female "smile and talk it out" works for everyone.

Some of us don't want—or need—to talk everything out.

When Maia was little and had been through a traumatic experience, I did what I thought was right: I encouraged her to talk about it. When she wouldn't talk to me, I took her to social workers, psychiatrists, and counselors who I thought would help her find the words she needed to communicate her ordeal and, in doing so, get the trauma out of her body. They questioned her. She didn't budge. And in the end, their interrogations—and mine—didn't do Maia any good. What helped, I can see now, was to leave her alone. What helped was getting her art supplies so she could draw dark and fiery landscapes. What helped was time. *Time.* What helped was allowing her to express herself in her own way and then let it go. She didn't want to dwell.

Many of us have been terrorized by legacies of forced silences in our families and our cultures. Our response, sometimes, has been to push too far in the other direction. But forcing someone to talk is no more helpful than forcing them to shut up. Interrogation can inspire aloofness. And according to new studies in that same world of psychiatry that taught us to rehash our every nightmare, those of us who minimize, repress, or consciously forget certain hurts may be better off.

In the aftermath of September 11, swarms of therapists descended on New York City—three for every victim, by some estimates. They came urging survivors to *talk*. They interviewed and reinterviewed them. What happened, according to trauma researchers, is that some of those survivors got worse. They didn't want to talk. They wanted to go to the beach. They wanted to spend time with their families. They wanted to stare at the skyline. They wanted to be quiet. They did not want some stranger shrink digging around in their fresh wounds.

Silence based on fear can be unhealthy, it's true. We all need to be *allowed* to express everything we are and to tell all the stories of our lives. As parents, we need to listen to our kids when they do speak up. But forcing every introvert to come up with words for her pain and harassing every trauma victim to revisit the scene of past horrors can be totally counterproductive. There is nothing wrong with mulling things over in the privacy of our own rooms and dreams.

Sometimes those Keep Out signs on our kids' doors just mean they need some alone time. Sometimes it means they're masturbating. Sometimes it means they're zoning out. Sometimes it means they're thinking things through and learning to deal with their own issues. Sometimes it means they're listening to music and distracting themselves from the harder parts of their lives. Sometimes it means they tend toward introversion and stoicism. All these things are OK. The good news is that most teenagers who are in real emotional trouble do speak up or show us in other ways that they need help. They'll leave a piece of writing lying around. Their desire for privacy will morph into secretiveness. Even without much talk, we can notice when our kids don't seem to be going through ups and downs, but only downs. When things get unbearable, even our introverts will usually let us know that they're in a crisis. So it's our job to listen to our kids and take the things they say seriously when they do want to talk, rather than freaking out; to ask directly what they're thinking or planning; to assess the immediate danger; to seek help if we need it; and to let them know that the lines of communication are always open. We're always willing to talk. If talking feels uncomfortable, we're willing to read a note. Parental operators are standing by.

In the meantime, we can nurture the emotional connections we do have with our kids, and honor the silences as much as we honor their expressiveness.

"What are you thinking about?" my daughter has gotten into the habit of asking me almost every day.

Usually, I tell her. Or I tell her a goodly portion of what I'm thinking. Sometimes, however, I prefer to keep my thoughts to myself. And so she lets it go. I'm learning, slowly, to extend her the same courtesy.

"I Am an Original"

I came across Miles online—he'd written a great article about making the transition from high school to higher ed—so I decided to drop him an e-mail.

A nineteen-year-old student at City College of San Francisco, Miles seemed like an eloquent guy who could enlighten me on the inner life of a teen boy.

Me: How would you describe your upbringing?
Miles: I lived with my mom for the first thirteen years of my life in a housing project in Albuquerque, New Mexico. My mom was an alcoholic and used drugs. I wish she would've been more of a parent, but I guess it's too late now. If I got out of line, she would let me know and punish me, but as far as maintaining a certain level of discipline all the time, there was none.

I met my dad for the first time in 1996, when I moved to San Francisco to live with him. I was always acting bad, and he'd always try to come at me with some kind of discipline bullshit, like if I acted up, I would get grounded, or not be able to turn on the TV. But none of that worked, because I was always acting bad, even after he punished me. I didn't want to be in San Francisco, I wanted to be back home with my mom. So really, it's like he did all that work for nothing.

When I look back on it, I probably would've done the same thing if my kid was acting up, so I don't really know how I feel about it. I know that I'm mad about him not giving me the freedom to stay with my mom while she was sick, and moving me across the country just because he chose to live in San Francisco.

Me: One thing I hear from a lot of parents, especially parents of teenage boys, is that communication gets difficult. Parents feel shut out. Do you have any insight into that?

Miles: That's basically the mentality of teenage boys is to shut out their parents, because really, at that point, they don't want them all in their business like that. At that age, when adolescent boys start becoming teenagers, they sometimes start using drugs and alcohol, or at least are prone to, and they don't want their parents to know that.

In the process, parents get shut out of more things than their child's drug activity. Basically, teenagers shut out their parents in order to keep themselves from getting in trouble, and in the meantime, parents lose touch with their children. It's just something that happens.

Me: Did you have any problems with drugs?

Miles: Nearly all the people I knew in high school, who weren't committed to a sport or a strenuous academic activity, used some kind of drug, mostly marijuana and alcohol. The kids who were doing anything more than that usually hung out in the back of the campus.

I'm not going to lie. I did my share of things in the past.

What do you expect? I'm young. Things like that are going to happen in a young person's life. It's all about how you deal with it. If you take one drink and then the next minute you're selling your blood for liquor, you have no business drinking alcohol in the first place. Me, I can do that stuff responsibly, so that's OK, but young people think that they can just do that stuff and act a fool and not have to suffer the consequences, and it's not like that. It never can become a priority. That's when everything goes bad. That hasn't even come close to happening to me.

Me: Did your parents worry about your personal safety as all of this was going on? How did that play out?
Miles: I know my mom worried about me and my sister a lot when we first moved to San Francisco, just because we were so far away.

I don't think my dad ever did, because at one point in high school, I was writing essays about killing myself, and just ending it all, and he didn't even care. I don't even think he knew about it, so that was probably the school's fault for not telling him. But if it was me, I would be able to tell off the top that something was wrong with my kid. But I guess that's just me.

Me: How did you get through that? Did anyone try to intervene or help you?
Miles: A few people tried to intervene. I can't say they really helped me.

The teacher who I turned the essay in for gave it to this counselor. All this guy really tried to do was get in my head, and me being young and impressionable, I sort of gave him an opening. But he didn't help me at all.

I was really feeling like I needed something, more importantly someone. I was really feeling alone, and I didn't want to feel that anymore, so I got attached to this girl who was in a lot of my classes. I can't even remember what drew me to her. I think it was mainly because she just said "hi" to me and smiled at me. I'd talk to her from time to time, and we'd do the e-mail thing, and every week I'd go tell the counselor about this. He'd just keep egging me on, making me believe this whole thing was real, and I was believing him, when she probably didn't even feel the same way.

After about two months she stopped answering her e-mails, talking about how her computer was broken. She didn't come to school for like a week, and I really started losing it. I came to school ready to kill myself. The counselor came at me asking me if I wanted to spend the weekend in a hospital, and I was like, "no," but then he told me it was too late, and a few seconds later I was in handcuffs going to a hospital.

I called the girl when I was in there, and it was like she hardly knew who I was, and when she hung up on me, I just started crying.

To say I was hurting during that period of time would be an understatement. The pain I was feeling was indescribable, but ultimately the only person who could get me through it was myself, and that was done when I realized that I have a greater purpose that would be denied by me to die at age sixteen.

I see the girl up at City College. She doesn't say a word to me, and I doubt she remembers me.

I say to myself now, "This is the person I was ready to kill myself over?"

I just realized, I can't go out like that, and there's more out there for me.

When it comes to death, there's no coming back from that, and I don't want to die knowing I have not lived my life to its fullest potential.

Me: It seems from your article that you've done very well academically. Are you naturally interested in academics?
Miles: I hope this is not a general question you planned to ask whoever, but I'll be honest with you, I'm not that talented in academics. I can make myself sound talented in academics, but really, when it comes to science and mathematics, I just barely make it by. I hate math, and I probably hate science even worse. I'm basically just a talented writer, and when it comes to things of that nature (literature, social studies, etc.), I'm the man. The only reason I got to give the graduation speech was because of my writing talent. It almost had nothing to do with how I gave the speech, it was just what I was saying. I'm not trying to sell myself short or anything, but there are people out here who are really smart. I'm just a writer, and that's enough for me. I definitely get that from my mom. I always remember her writing in her journal, no matter how out of it she was. That is definitely something that she passed down to me, and I thank her for that.

Me: In what other ways did your parents' attitudes influence you?
Miles: My mom's attitude was mostly being drunk, but slightly free-spirited, because she used to be a "hippie" back in the '60s. My dad was more of the same.

My mother passed away when I was fifteen, in 1997. I think that ultimately what killed her was the fact that she would never see me and my sister again, and I think she knew that when we moved to San Francisco. I blame that entirely on my dad.

I feel that my life would be a lot different if she would've been with me through middle and high school, and maybe I would've been more successful. Because I have had to learn to survive in this world without a mother's love, I missed out on opportunities I could've capitalized on.

I'll always love my mother, and I hope she was listening at my high school graduation when I dedicated my speech to her, because not only was that speech dedicated to her, but my whole life up to this point is dedicated to her memory.

My mom influenced me in a sense of being a free spirit, but mostly, I am an original. My strongest influence is myself, and I wouldn't have it any other way.

The Color of Growing Up

I asked fifteen- and sixteen-year-olds, "What color is childhood?"

Yellow
Baby blue
Bright orange
Pastels
Pink and blue
Rose and lilac
Pink and purple
The colors of summer
Light yellow
Green because you're always playing outside
Black and white
A rainbow
Anything bright
The color of alfalfa fields
Like cartoons

"And what color is adolescence?"

Black
Red
Black and purple painted stripes
Cherry
China red
Red-orange
Red like my new car. Unstoppable
Yellow ringed with red
The color of fire
Gray
Transparent
The color of a shooting star
Fireworks against a night sky
Royal blue
Midnight blue
Sea blue
Navy blue
Blue. All colors of blue. You're lost in an
ocean of blue. Darker shades in the deep
parts. In the dark you struggle, trying to
stay afloat. The salt water stings.

That Has Made
Me Stronger

I asked a group of teenagers to describe the make-or-break crisis of
their life . . .

*A big change that affected my life was deciding if I wanted to live
with my mom or my dad after they got a divorce about a year
ago and my dad moved into a different house. My mom and the
rest of my brothers and sisters stayed in our house. I had to
decide which parent I wanted to live with. They said it was my
choice. I decided to live with my mom, since she did live in the
house I grew up in. I spend every weekend over at my dad's
house. Everything's worked out OK.*

—Dominica, 17

*After my brother passed away, I started doing badly in school. I
got bad grades and was pushing my friends away. I didn't feel
like doing anything. My life started to turn around when my
friends didn't give up on me. They were there by my side when I*

didn't want them to be, and comforted me when I needed to be comforted. My friends were the ones that helped me get through it.

—Kim, 16

Freshman year I was failing English. I knew I could get my grade back up if I tried, but my parents had very little confidence in me, so they kept nagging and nagging which was making it even harder to concentrate on the goal ahead of me. After long hard work, I brought my grade back up to a C+. The point is that as long as you are confident in yourself, it doesn't matter what other people think.

—Nick, 15

When I found out that I was six weeks pregnant, the first thing that came out of my parents' mouths was "You're keeping it." I knew it was my choice and that I didn't have to keep the baby, but it seemed easier just to listen to them. People in our family don't have abortions. See, abortion is a sin in their eyes. Only if I'd known what I know now, I wouldn't have cared what they thought or said. I would have had the abortion. Having a kid is a lot harder than I would have ever thought it would be. Nothing against my son. I love him to death, but I truly wasn't ready.

—Tylena, 17

About a year ago, my stepbrother opened up a shop down in Mississippi. He asked me if I wanted to work for him. I would get paid 100 dollars a day. I was behind in one of my classes. I could use the money I had for summer school or for a plane ticket to Mississippi. I was so excited about going to work for my brother, but then I started to think: Money or education? In the end, I chose education—my future depends on it. I can work next summer.

—Kevin, 15

Has anyone ever asked you to choose between him or her and your family? Well, they have me and it seemed like a hard decision and an awkward thing to ask a friend. If I chose my friend over my family, she would be happy, but I felt like I was disbanding myself of my words—I'd always said I was a "family girl." So I thought about it more: If I chose my family, I'd feel good and true, and maybe my friend would understand. My family is all I need and all I have. Like they say in the Lilo and Stitch movie, Ohana means family, and family means nobody gets left behind.

—"Lilo," 15

I lost all four of my grandparents and my great-uncle in a five-year period. I was very close to each one and it was hard for me to grasp the fact that they were gone. Though this time was difficult, my parents helped me realize that even though people die, their spirits are still with us. That has made me stronger.

—Redmond, 15

Decision making is so hard. A big decision I had to make was whether to abort or have my baby. I was only in the ninth grade. I took it upon myself to have sex when I wasn't supposed to. When I found out I was pregnant, I was so scared 'cause I didn't know what to do. I wasn't ready for a baby. I was only a baby myself.

—"Miss Chocolate," 17

Lock Them In or Lock Them Out?

Here are two time-honored traditional reactions to having a teenager:

1. lock them in the house, or

2. lock them out of the house.

One friend won't let her daughter out of her sight. "The world is full of mean, bad people," she says. Until now, this mom has managed to keep her clan sheltered from that world—energetically homeschooling them for fourteen years. But now her oldest is begging to go to the local high school. And my friend says, "No way—I mean, *high school*. What could be worse?"

I pick up a popular book on parenting adolescents. It opens with a story about an older teen getting picked up by the police for the first time. The father decides not to bail him out. This, according to the authors, is the right response. *Let the kid learn a lesson in jail.* And I'm reminded of a friend's parents from my own teen years: They practiced "tough love" by locking their kids out on cold nights. Often, their tough-loved daughter ended up sleeping on my bedroom floor. In the morning, she'd spark up a joint, inhale deeply, hold her breath, then exhale a thick cloud of smoke. "My parents," she'd say, "are *such* ass-holes." Lesson learned.

Both parental responses are understandable. I, too, want to protect my girl-woman from the mean, bad people in the world. The wicked paradox of parenting teens is that we need to learn to let go at the very time when our children's lives can be the most dangerous, and the consequences for screwing up most life-altering. I also want my daughter to learn her own lessons. I want her to fly. But if she falls, I want to be there to catch her. (I also want a vacation home in Ibiza, and Emma Goldman alive and in the White House. *Sigh.*)

But here's the deal: Neither response works. Locking our kids out of the house may be our right as parents, but unless the kid is armed and dangerous (in which case we probably have to call the cops), I think it's ridiculous. If things are so bad at home that we need to move our kids out, it's our responsibility to make sure they have another safe place to live. County jails and city streets are not safe places to live.

We can't keep our children prisoners, either. What would they do when they finally got out at eighteen, anyway? Our kids need to learn to deal with the world—mean, bad people and all.

We can, however, keep track of everyone in our family. The biggest difference I see between teenagers now and the hooligans I hung out with in the '80s is that these days, kids are a lot less likely to be unsupervised or unaccounted for. They're in afterschool programs. They're at friends' houses we know. They're at the mall armed with cell phones. In 1983, that famous public-service announcement "It's 10 P.M., do you know where your children are?" was such a joke. But by 10 P.M. in 2003, most of us have a pretty good idea. We also often know where our partners, roommates, and close friends are. We keep track of each other. And that's all right.

Fat and Imaginary Fat

It's lunchtime. A kid scarfs down two burgers and a super-size order of fries, slurps a giant soda. After school, he'll head home to sit in front of the TV and consume another thousand empty calories.

Another child appears to be enjoying several slices of pizza, a bag of cheese chips, and a strawberry milkshake. Later she'll excuse herself to the bathroom, stick her finger down her throat, and force herself to vomit.

A third teen sips a diet soda from a straw and picks at her dressing-less salad. She says she isn't hungry. Actually, she's starving.

According to the Centers for Disease Control and Prevention, some 20% of American teenagers are heavy enough to be considered obese. And the National Association of Anorexia Nervosa and Associated Disorders estimates that one in every seven females between the ages of twelve and twenty-five develops bulimia, while one in every hundred suffers from anorexia. Men and boys develop eating disorders, too, but less frequently, accounting for about 10% of all cases. That's a whole lot of youngsters courting dangerous relationships with food and their own bodies, and it adds up to a whole lot of despair.

We are a nation obsessed with thinness, and also the country with the worst nutritional habits in the world. If our kids watch TV and consume other media, they're deluged with images of gaunt women and buffed men. In between shows featuring starving actors and genetic oddities, junk-food marketers push oversized servings of sugar juice and deep-fried starch. It's all part of a Western lifestyle in which we've collectively become so complacent—even arrogant—about being able to feed ourselves that we've at once forgotten about basic nutrition and developed an ideal of female beauty that suggests the brink of starvation.

Genetics, stress, hormones, puberty, brain-chemistry changes, and other factors contribute to our weight and our tendency toward eating disorders, but television—that great purveyor of Western culture—also plays a huge role. Studies have shown that TV viewing is the second most pivotal predictor of teen obesity (the first being childhood weight problems based on heredity, diet, and, yes, more television).

Eating disorders can also be linked to media influence. Fiji, an island nation where bodacious bods were traditionally appreciated, was struck by an outbreak of anorexia and bulimia after the arrival of television in 1995.

Anne Becker, an anthropologist who studied Fijian eating habits, compared the arrival of TV with that of nineteenth-century British explorers who brought with them a devastating plague of measles. In 1998—three years after the Fijian TV station went on the air—Becker conducted a survey of teenage girls and found that 74% now considered themselves "too big or fat" and the number of girls with eating disorders had jumped by 400%.

So what's really "too big or fat"?

You can look up height and weight on the body mass index— either online or in most books on nutrition—but here's a more basic formula: If you and your kids are eating two to four balanced and reasonably sized meals a day, avoiding most junk food and sugars, and exercising about three times a week, you're doing just fine. When looking at height-weight charts, remember that these things don't take into account that muscle weighs more than fat, or that there are millions of beautiful body shapes and we all have one have one.

As for diet and nutrition, most teens get plenty of protein, but can lag when it comes to fruit, veggies, and whole grains. Sugar and junk food can tweak their blood-sugar levels and confuse their bodies about how much food they really need. We may not get much say in what our kids eat when they're not with us, but we can make sure we've got healthy snacks and good meals available when they're home.

If you're short on cash, you might be surprised to discover that you don't have to be destitute to qualify for Food Stamps. For example, as a working parent with one kid, I can get Food Stamps in Oregon any month my income falls below about eighteen hundred dollars. There's no harm in heading over to your local social services office to find out if you qualify, too.

As parents, we can also make sure our kids have access to nutrition information beyond what they might find in teen magazines or Internet sites that actually encourage anorexia and provide forums with tips for extreme weight loss (I am not joking). While eating disorders can sneak up on some people, many kids actually hear about anorexia and bulimia and then consciously cultivate the disorders, thinking they'll be able to use them for crash diets.

Kaz Cooke's *Real Gorgeous: The Truth about Body and Beauty* is a radical, teen-friendly book chock-full of nutrition reality and body-acceptance wisdom. Put it on your kid's desk. For teens who'd rather not have a pink tome that also includes lots of information on makeup and breasts, I'd go for the gender-neutral *Fueling the Teen Machine*, by Ellen Shanley and Colleen Thompson. The online *Beauty Magazine* (www.beautymagazine.ca) is one young Canadian woman's awesome response to the mainstream beauty industry's attempted hijacking of her brain, and a good source for stories and information about recovering from an eating disorder.

All my life I have been overweight . . . and all my life my mother has made a point to point it out to me, as if being fat in a fat-phobic society wasn't enough. I used to wish I had an eating disorder. I remember binging on food and then sitting in front of the toilet sobbing and wishing that I could make myself throw up. Visions of diets and gym memberships and my "big plans" to lose weight all through high school, and even now in my second year of college, permeate my thoughts. My mother continues to nag me, and embarrass me and make me feel like no matter how smart I am, no matter how self-sufficient and brilliant and wonderful I am, it won't matter because I am fat, and fat girls just don't make it in this world. Too bad I'm smarter than that.

—Lindsey, 19

In junior high school I shifted from being interested in keeping fit, to being obsessed with losing weight. Fascinated with the eating-disorder videos I was shown in gym class, I slowly started restricting and regimenting my diet. I went to the gym as well as

my dance classes. I did not have a life; I had an eating disorder.
Nothing else mattered to me but my planned diet and exercise
regime for the day. . . . Food restrictions and bizarre eating
habits distort the mind. Beneath the obsession with weight,
appearance, and calories lies a deep complexity of pain. Beneath
what seemed like superficial airs, powerful beauty lay concealed
in self-disgust.

—Lori, 21

When kids show signs of real trouble with food and body image—
sudden, extreme weight loss, vomiting, fat that seems unhealthy, or
major weight fluctuations—there's no need for us to get accusatory or
start nagging. While nutrition talk is nothing to shy away from,
parental comments that focus on a kid's body or weight can be more
harmful than helpful. Still, we can get them to an eating-disorder spe-
cialist, acupuncturist, nutritionist, pediatrician, or naturopath for some
help and advice. Without treatment, up to 20% of kids with serious
eating disorders will die. With treatment, the mortality rate falls to
about 2%—and full recovery can be expected for about 60%.
Acupuncture in conjunction with other health care may be particularly
helpful, as traditional Chinese health care can calm the mind and heart
while treating metabolic and appetite imbalances. And any doctor or
nurse's explanation of a healthy diet and expression of concern will be
a lot more effective than Mom or Dad's *blah blah blah.* I'd been begging Maia to eat a proper breakfast for months when, one morning, I
walked into the kitchen to find her toasting a bagel.

"Yum," I said.

"Yeah," she half-sighed. "The school nurse told me I had to eat
breakfast every morning."

"Well, I guess it's a good idea then."

We can take it from the school nurse. And we can take it from Kaz Cooke: "There are millions of gorgeous body shapes. Yours is one of them. Dieting doesn't work. Your thighs are pretty cute. Exercise should be fun. Plastic surgery sucks. Modeling can be miserable. You can recover from an eating disorder. You can read magazines and watch television critically. You can fight the body police."

Suicide

I was suicidal just because it felt right somehow. I got off in walking that line and just stepping back after looking over the edge of death. I felt cradled by morbid things, and suicide is as morbid as it comes.

—David, 19

I've been procrastinating writing about teenage suicide. I could leave it out. There are a lot of topics I've passed over because I know you can find the information easily online or in any number of other books. But I'm tempted to leave this one out for a different reason: It scares me. To invoke suicide seems almost ominous. It's that deep a taboo.

Teen suicide is less common than most of us imagine—and the rates are declining—but suicide remains one of the leading causes of death in young people, and a parent's greatest fear. Like the fatal drunk-driving accident or overdose, it's the tragedy our kids can't recover from. We can handle just about anything, *except* outliving our children. And somehow suicide feels like the worst way we could outlive them. We understand that they could get cancer. We understand that they could die in some freak accident. We even understand car crashes. But suicide? It's the nagging fear that lurks at the edges of so many of our fleeting worries. Particularly unbearable because we feel it's preventable. Particularly tragic because we feel sure whatever suffering prompted it could have been healed in life. Particularly frightening because we know that the younger the suicidal individual, the less *time* they are likely to have spent considering their choice.

But not talking about suicide doesn't make the fear or the possibility go away. Followers of religions that strongly prohibit suicide, like Christianity and Islam, actually have higher suicide rates than followers of religions that have no strong prohibition, like Buddhism and Hinduism. Taboo is no deterrent.

So let's deal with it.

Only about one in nine thousand kids between the ages of ten and nineteen commits suicide each year. The rate for adults is much higher. Your partner, your best friend, and your own mother are all more likely to take their own lives. Your father is *significantly* more likely to take his own life. Still, some two thousand American teens do kill themselves every year. And another two hundred thousand *attempt* to.

Suicide is reported as the second-leading cause of death in fifteen- to twenty-four-year-olds, exceeded only by traffic accidents. So this is serious, especially when we consider that many teenage suicides are "of-the-moment" responses to immediate problems our kids see no solution for.

Girls are slightly more inclined to attempt suicide, but boys are actually four times as likely to *die* as a result of an attempt. The truth behind this statistic is that a girl's weapon of choice is more likely to be pills, while a boy is more apt to use a firearm.

Any child might consider suicide—the knowledge and reality that we have the power to end our own lives is part of the extraordinary magic of being human—but some teens are more vulnerable than others. Boys already suffering from emotional or behavioral disorders, gays and lesbians, kids who use alcohol or other drugs, kids with easy access to potentially lethal medications or firearms, kids who have recently lost a friend or relative to suicide, and kids with histories of violence and suicide attempts are all at higher risk than the rest of the population.

Sometimes there aren't many warning signs, but many vulnerable kids will actually identify themselves to us without being asked: They are the kids who talk about wanting to die. They break the taboo, they bring up the subject we've been trying to avoid, and, sometimes, because *we* don't want to deal with it, they get ignored. As often happens with homicidal kids, the desperation, threats, and stated plans sometimes get written off as melodrama. *They can't mean it,* we tell ourselves. We don't want to be paranoid, so we ignore even our own intuition. We imagine that people who talk about suicide are not really the ones who go through with it. But research shows us this: Teens who took their own lives often told their parents *repeatedly*—verbally or in writing—that they intended to kill themselves. They talked about suicide, sometimes jokingly. They threatened suicide. They *attempted* suicide. They said things like "I want to die," "Nothing matters," "I don't care anymore," "Everyone would be better off without me," and "You won't have to worry about me for much longer." All of these comments—and our own gut feelings—need to be taken seriously. Not all verbalized thoughts of suicide are serious, but it is a myth that people who talk about killing themselves don't really attempt it.

*When I was fifteen, I'd been cutting myself and I told my mom I
was going to commit suicide. She said, "Go ahead, if that's what
you really want!" I guess she'd reached her breaking point. But at
the time it just made me feel even more worthless and hopeless.
She was the only person who I thought really loved me and would
be there for me no matter what. After that I knew I had no one.*

—Lucinda, 19

As parents dealing with our teens' emotional problems, we do reach a
breaking point. So it's incredibly important for us to be taking care of
ourselves, too. We may feel heroically selfless as we try intervention
after intervention, but if we don't take time to deal with our own frustration and fatigue, resentment can bubble up and spew out of us at
the exact wrong (and pivotal) moment. I do not know Lucinda's
mother, but I am convinced that she did not mean what she said.
Lucinda, to this day, believes that she meant it.

*I think I was sixteen. I would get out my stepdad's gun when I
was home alone, and I would just hold it to my head, thinking
how much better everything would be if I just pulled the trigger.
One time I told my mom what I was going to do. At first she just
got really upset and told me not to say anything like that and
didn't I appreciate everything, but later that night she came into
my room and asked me about it, just really calmly, and she told
me how much she loved me and how much she would miss me.
After that she took me to counseling. I hadn't mentioned the gun
to her, but the next time I went out to get it, it was just gone. I
guess she made my stepdad get rid of it.*

—Anthony, 21

If our kids do talk about wanting to die, or if we have an intuition that they are moving toward taking drastic, self-destructive, or violent action, we can set aside our own panic and taboos and ask them directly what they are thinking. We can absolutely get rid of any potentially lethal medications or firearms in the house. And we can get some outside help. Talk therapy is often super-helpful for kids dealing with snowballing despair. Family therapy is probably not a bad idea. Antidepressant medication, though often prescribed, should be used only with *extreme* caution. Paxil has already been shown to triple the risk of adolescent suicide, and I won't be surprised when other selective serotonin reuptake inhibitors get added to the list of drugs considered dangerous for teens.

In an emergency situation, we can call a suicide hotline and talk to people who deal with similar crises every day. If our kids are already under the care of a mental-health professional, we can alert them, or we can find a good counselor in our community. If we have the sense that our kids may try to hurt themselves, we can also refuse to leave them alone. None of us wants to be paranoid, but no one's going to fault us for erring on the side of caution here.

With intervention, the desire to take one's own life typically fades within a few hours or days. We won't have to be on suicide watch forever. But we can take these crises seriously, refuse to let our own panic rule the day, and do our best to help our kids through.

Uncle Sam Is a Pusher

Maybe you've noticed all the glamorous commercials on TV, or the slick brochures that have started arriving in the mail addressed to your child, or the suave radio ads on the hip-hop stations—all promising opportunity and adventure to ambitious youngsters. Uncle Sam wants your teenager.

As I write this, the draft has not been reinstated. Even as the prospect of another massive long-term war looms, the military is filling its ranks with "volunteer" troops.

With sophisticated marketing techniques, inflated promises of college financial aid, the allure of exciting travel, and new laws requiring public schools to hand over student records, the Pentagon plans to lure more and more of our kids into military life.

Targeting low-income youth with high-pressure sales pitches and loads of promises, the military has kept up its supply of ground troops for the past several decades. Under W's administration, recruiters gained even broader access to American teenagers. Buried deep within the No Child Left Behind Act, Bush Jr.'s sweeping education law passed in 2002, is a provision requiring public secondary schools to provide military recruiters not only with access to facilities, but also with contact information for every student.

Undercutting the authority of some local school districts, including San Francisco and Portland, Oregon, that had previously barred recruiters from schools on the grounds that the military discriminates against gays and lesbians, this law gives the military unfettered access to our kids. Recruiters—military salespeople with quotas to meet—are up-front about their plans to use the school lists to aggressively pursue students through mailings, phone calls, and personal visits, *even if parents object.*

Once our kids enlist, they become the property of the military. If their experience doesn't live up to the advertising, they can't bring their enlistment agreement back to the recruiter for a refund. They're in it for eight years.

The military promises job training and money for college. Too bad the promises are often empty. Becoming a soldier is not a "way out" for low-income kids. While the military advertises financial aid, two-thirds of recruits never get a cent—and only 15% graduate with a four-year degree. According to a report in the *Army Times,* the military actually took $720 million more from GIs in nonrefundable deposits than it paid out in college benefits between 1986 and 1993.

Nor is the military an effective job-training program. Only 12% of male veterans and 6% of female veterans report using skills learned in the military in their current jobs. According to the Department of Veterans Affairs, veterans overall earn less than nonveterans. And once someone has spent a few years in the military, he's two to five times more likely to be homeless than his friends who never joined. As Dick Cheney said when he was secretary of defense, "The reason to have a military is to be prepared to fight and win wars. . . . It's not a jobs program."

For women recruits, life in the military can be hell. Sexual harassment and assault are daily realities. The VA's own figures show 90% of recent women veterans reported suffering harassment, and 30% reported having been raped.

And for people of color—aggressively targeted by recruiters—the military represents a truly dead-end career. During the Gulf War, more than half of frontline troops were people of color. Overall, about a third of enlisted personnel (but only 12% of officers) are people of color. When recent studies showed a slight dip in young African Americans' interest in the military, the Pentagon reacted with a new campaign targeting Latino youth with Spanish-language ads. The recruiters' lethal result: tracking high-achieving young people in communities of color into a deadly occupation.

So, what's the most effective recruitment tool for enticing young soldiers? It's the Junior Reserve Officer Training Corps—or JROTC—a class offered to middle and high school students across the country. Kids as young as eleven who have nowhere else to go, who don't make it into honors classes, who don't "fit in" to drama, debating, chorus, or activism clubs wind up in JROTC. Colin Powell has called the program a sort of "good gang."

According to its website, JROTC offers students a wealth of opportunities:

> *Motivating and developing young people is what JROTC is all about. To accomplish this goal, it combines classroom instruction and extracurricular activities oriented on* [sic] *attaining an*

awareness of the rights, responsibilities, and privileges of citizenship; developing the student's (cadet's) sense of personal responsibility; building life skills; and providing leadership opportunities.

What you study in Junior ROTC isn't found in any textbook. It won't be studied by any other students or in any other schools. It hasn't been taught before and it won't be taught again. Because the subject of JROTC is—YOU. JROTC is all about you. You are its whole point. It's devoted to your growth, both as a student and as a person.

Sounds all right, doesn't it? Even kind of exciting? Too bad it's a ploy. In reality, students learn to obey orders. The Army JROTC text states that "When troops react to command rather than thought, the result is more than just a good-looking ceremony or parade. Drill has been and will continue to be the backbone of military discipline." And the Navy JROTC text prescribes "[l]oyalty to those above us in the chain of command, whether or not we agree with them."

This isn't a leadership program devoted to a student's personal growth, it's a course in mindless obedience to authoritarian control.

Instead of offering an alternative to violence, JROTC brings guns into the schools. The curriculum glorifies war, trains students to fire rifles and pistols, and teaches a skewed version of military history. Here's an example from the Army JROTC textbook: "Fortunately for the Army, the government policy of pushing the Indians farther west then wiping them out was carried out successfully."

In addition to celebrating racism, JROTC textbooks ignore women's contributions to history. And veterans with disabilities are excluded from receiving the Pentagon authorization required to become a JROTC instructor. *Wouldn't want to show kids what really happens when you go to war.*

While there's no requirement that JROTC students serve on active duty, about 50% of all program graduates do enter the military. By the end of their eight years of duty, there's no guarantee they'll be alive, no guarantee they'll be able to go to college, no guarantee they'll be better qualified for a civilian job—and certainly no guarantee they won't be suffering from some "mystery disease" like Gulf War and Vietnam War veterans who were exposed to chemical weapons.

As the Central Committee for Conscientious Objectors puts it, "The military is hazardous to our lives. . . . The 'adventure' in the commercials is code for war, the 'discipline' code for violence. The military trains recruits to employ deadly force."

What can we do? If our kids are learning about the military from recruiters alone, they're getting only a small part of the story. Do we let the pusher on the corner be our children's sole source for drug information? Of course we don't. Just as we talk to our kids about drugs and sex, we need to educate ourselves and teach our teenagers the truth about military life: the dehumanizing process of basic training, the psychological costs of killing, and the horrors of war. Contact the Central Committee for Conscientious Objectors for resources and current information (see the back of this book).

We may not have to help our kids dodge the draft. But if recruiters get hold of our teenagers' imaginations, we've got our work cut out for us.

Why Do I Bother?

Talk to parents of teenagers, and they're bound to lament that their kids aren't listening to them. We feel like the grownups in the *Peanuts* cartoons: *Wah wah wah wah, wah wah wah* . . . So I asked a group of thirty- and forty-something folks what they remembered from their own teen years: Tell me about something that was said to you as a teenager that had a lasting impact on your life. The answers were disquieting. Almost everyone remembered something negative a parent told them:

I wanted to be a model and my dad told me I was too fat. Six months later I was in the hospital at eighty pounds. But I didn't want to be a model anymore.

My mom told me she wished I would disappear. And I think I did it. Right then, I think I disappeared. Emotionally, socially, and within our relationship, I really disappeared. I don't know where I went. I've spent years now trying to find where I went.

*My father told me, "Michael Jordan would never marry someone
like you." I remember feeling that he didn't think much of me. I
still struggle with that in my personal relationships.*

*I was having a hard time in school and my mom said I was lazy.
I believed her. Even years later, whenever something wasn't
happening for me, I'd think,* Oh, it's because I'm lazy, *and I'd go
back to bed.*

*I wanted a black leather miniskirt, and Mother told me it would
make me look like the cow it came off of. I remember that
comment dashing any possibility of acceptance of my body I had
at that point. It took me years to tell her how hurtful that had
been, and she didn't even remember having said it.*

Certainly there were positive comments, too—hopeful and encouraging
words we gathered up and used to craft our identities. But the vast
majority of the people I asked reported that those comments came
from teachers or stepparents:

*My sophomore English teacher told me I was a great writer. After
I had struggled through algebra and chemistry, his kind words
made me feel like I was actually good at something! Writing
feverishly for the last two years of high school, I found an outlet
for all my teen angst.*

*In ninth grade everyone was telling me that these were the best
years of my life. I was depressed. I figured that if these were my
"best years," I might as well kill myself. My stepfather had a talk*

with me one afternoon. He told me to tough it out: Things would get better. In college I could choose my own classes, I'd be getting laid, I could sleep till noon if I wanted to. He affirmed that my life was tough and made it clear that it would be better in the future. He gave me the strength to suffer through.

When I was seventeen, my high school history teacher asked me what I was going to do after graduation. I shrugged. I had no plans. She frowned and said, "You need to go to college." When I mumbled something about the whole prospect being too difficult and expensive, she shook her head and pulled out a brochure for a state school with an interdisciplinary curriculum. She tapped the brochure and told me that I had to go, that there was no other option.

My ninth-grade English teacher gave me the "you can do whatever you set your mind to" speech, and it really made me believe that. She was a hard teacher, a strong and respected woman, and I was so pleased to get her praise and encouragement that I rose to the occasion.

So where were all the loving and encouraging mothers? Did everyone I talked to really have such jerk-butts for primary caregivers? Or do teenagers hear only the *negative* things their parents tell them? Maybe as teens, we figure our parents are supposed to praise us, so we let their unexpected insults cut us and only believe words of encouragement from teachers and other authority figures. It's disheartening as hell to think that I might spend my daughter's teen years praising everything I see in her that is amazing and inspiring, only to have her latch on to one stupid thing that slips out of my mouth when I'm tired. In hopes of hearing something a little more promising, I went back to my little survey group, begged them to think of one single positive thing their mothers said to them when they were teenagers. But most everyone drew a blank, stared at me, then switched gears and started waxing philosophical about all that their mothers had done for them:

Oh, don't get me wrong. My mother was awesome. She raised me, dressed me, loved me. Everything I am can be credited to her— but it was so all-encompassing, I didn't see it until much later. Now I think that the distinctive messages I received from other people were just like billboards in a desert, while my mother was the real oasis.

The positive things other people told me were things my mother had probably said herself, but I don't really remember a specific incident or a specific quote. Maybe her confidence in me allowed me to hear the good things my teachers told me? I guess she was more of a foundation.

My mother has always been supportive. It's harder to think of a single instance, though. I'll think some more about it.

Small solace, all this. I sure wish I knew how to meditate and be super-Zen and selfless. *Awesome? An oasis? A foundation?* What is all this vague shit?

I wish I knew how to be at peace with the fact that I will get no freakin' credit. I mean, what's the point? Why do I spend all my energy being the best mom I can be on any given day? Why do I bother? I mean, really. What is the point? Why am I cooking dinner? Why am I working my ass off so she can take a bunch of money to the vacuum of commercialism known as the mall? Why am I not at the beach? She's going to feel abandoned whether I do it or not, right? I want to go to the beach or I want some credit. One or the other!

And then, of course, I remember the point: We have children because mothering is good for the soul.

The problem is the point.

We will get no credit. But here's the thing: We'll do it anyway. Not because we're martyrs, but because it's good for the soul, good for *our* souls as well as our children's. We'll do it because our kids are amazing and we want to see them reach their full potential. And if somewhere in the process we manage to be a foundation, an oasis—vaguely "awesome" or "supportive"—all the better. But it turns out that my daughter isn't the only one who has some growing up left to do. I'm growing up, too. I'm learning to do what I believe in, to act in a way that I'll be proud of, to do my work in the world and in my family without expecting an Academy Award. I'm learning not to sit around waiting for a thank-you. Because here's what's true: She owes me nothing. Not even a thank-you. *She owes me nothing.* I'm gonna write that on a Post-it Note and stick it on my bedroom wall, because by this time tomorrow, I'll probably be all wound up in self-pity again.

God, I hate growing up.

Things That Keep *Me* Up at Night

Maia Swift

Night is my best time for thinking—I think for most people it is.
No, not my "best time," but I *think* the most at night. I usually
think about social stuff. Him: my new crush, what about that?
Does he like me? Wait! Does he know me? I heard he likes
Mary . . . *Maybe he thinks my name is Mary!* Maybe not. I don't
like Mary, I never have. Well, OK—I don't really know her, but I
don't have a reason to like her, and he might like her—so I don't.

Not only that—if that doesn't seem like much, it is to me—
but I also think about . . . hmm, friends at school. Marie, Alcina,
or just anyone. Maybe something I'm jealous of, someone, stuff
like that. I try and try not to be jealous, I hate jealousy! But, I am.

What about my family? What's going through my mom's
head right now? Maybe something bad about me. Maybe
nothing about me. I wonder if she's going to check up on me
tonight, hmm.

Deon is always at the park by my house real real late at night
like this—I can see him from my window . . . I bet I could get

away with it. Maybe not. I'm bad at that. I bet Mary's at the park right now.

I always turn on the radio while I go to sleep—what if someone dedicates that new "slow-jam" to me. Maybe not. But maybe. I'm lazy—why bother. Oh, shit, I forgot to turn on my alarm. Okay, I'm lazy, but I guess I can go out of my way to do it. Oh, no—the phone.

"Hello?" It's him. Why did he call? (I knew it wasn't Mary!) I like today.

But, what else keeps me up at night? My dad—of course my dad, who I haven't seen since I was eight. What's he doing? It's like . . . noon where he is, right? What's he doing? I wonder if he's thinking about me right now, if he has this whole day. Probably. My dad—I probably think about him more than anyone or anything. There's so much to think about!

I love him so much. (By the way—this essay goes out to him from now on.)

When I was younger I thought at night about how it would be so cool if I was adopted! Even more if I had a long-lost clone or twin, but that was stupid. I always tried to make myself believe it was true—that I was adopted. It's not like I didn't like my parents, but to have some kind of Lifetime movie drama in your life . . . Adopted—that would never work. When you put my mom and dad side by side, there's no way that I'm not their child. Got this from my mom, this from my dad, it's a perfect blend if you ask me. What about my dad's other kids? They don't look like me. What are they doing now? I wonder when I will see him. What would I say?

What about tomorrow? What's going to happen? Anything? Of course something, but what? Good, bad? Both. And after tomorrow? My future—what if things don't go exactly how I want them to? It's my life—I should have control, right? Every decision comes together, right? What if I make too many wrong ones? One too many could make the difference, right? Even one. One decision. Try not to think about it. Try not to think about it. Suddenly, I'm not thinking about anything. *Buona notte.*

Time Moving Forward

Two quick and easy ways of growing old are (1) to resist change obstinately and (2) to worship it abjectly. In the first case, we are caught like snags in a river, worn down and bleached by the flow of experience. In the second, we are fatigued and wrinkled by innumerable reorchestrations to circumstance. Those who remain fresh and vital, as though they floated in time, are people . . . who retain the youthful mechanism of converting change into growth.

—Robert Grudin, *Time and the Art of Living*

My Daughter Doesn't Think I Am a Shithead Anymore

My daughter doesn't think I am a shithead anymore.

As of the first of this month, my teenage daughter doesn't think I am a shithead!

No, my daughter thinks I'm "cool"! She thinks I'm funny. She wants me to take her and her friends to the mall. She doesn't want me to walk three yards behind her. She puts her arm around me while shopping for Hello Kitty watches!

I want to broadcast this news from the rooftops: "My daughter doesn't think I am a shithead anymore!"

I start climbing the nearest fire escape toward the nearest rooftop. I'm racking my brain trying to figure out what I've done right. Maybe if I can figure it out, I'll be able to put it in my book and everyone else can do the same thing and *their* children won't think *they're* shitheads anymore, either, and all will be well in the universe.

My daughter doesn't think I am a shithead anymore, and now I can save *all* the parents from the heartbreak of having a child who thinks her parent's a shithead!

Up, up, up I climb.

As I'm approaching the rooftop—still unclear as to what I've done to turn this whole "shithead" dynamic around—I remember a little something from a book I read a few months ago.

See, I have this penchant for buying self-help books at airport bookstores. It's hard for me to concentrate on a novel or an academic tome when I'm on a plane, but I can handle New Age inspiration. I think it mitigates a subconscious fear of flying. Anyway, a few transcontinental flights ago, I bought myself a copy of *The Four Agreements*. A cheesy little book, to be sure, with an unnaturally happy fellow smiling off the back cover. Still, in between takeoff and roasted peanuts, I started reading. By page four, I was hooked.

I wanted to be a Toltec warrior, too!

I could commit to these four agreements, I decided, and everything in my life would suddenly transform itself—I'd step into my destiny and become the glorious and worthy daughter of heaven I was always meant to be. Yes, *The Four Agreements* helped me a great deal on that springtime flight. My daughter thought I was a shithead at the time and author Don Miguel Ruiz had made me promise not to take these things personally. He'd cautioned me: "Whatever happens around you, don't take it personally. . . . If I see you on the street and I say, 'Hey, you are so stupid,' without knowing you, it's not about you; it's about me. If you take it personally, then perhaps you believe you are stupid. Maybe you think to yourself, 'How does he know? Is he clairvoyant, or can everybody see how stupid I am?' . . . Personal importance, or taking things personally, is the maximum expression of selfishness because we make the assumption that everything is about 'me.'"

I finally reach the last rung of the fire escape and crawl onto the gravelly rooftop. Making myself comfortable, I think, *Oh, come on, Don Miguel, I understand about not taking* negative *things personally, but my daughter doesn't think I am a shithead anymore. Can't I take this one thing personally? Doesn't this mean I'm a good person after all?*

It's like the way I feel after reading reviews of my own books. I get incredibly crabby and heartbroken and freaked out when someone says in black-and-white print that I've got no depth of character, or that I'm a pathetic pig-nut mother. I want to call up the reviewers and defend myself. I want to say, "When's the last time *you* put *your* heart in a book and told your truth to a bunch of strangers, you little shithead?!" And then when I read a good review, I get all pumped up, like this is just *it*. Like I'm suddenly worthy. Like my life is suddenly meaningful because some stranger reviewer person enjoyed my book and is waxing poetic about how great I am.

In other words, I'm not doing all that well with my four agreements.

I sit dumbly on the gravel rooftop. My daughter doesn't think I am a shithead anymore. This makes me happy, but I know it doesn't mean she won't think I am a shithead next month. It doesn't even mean that I am *not* a shithead. I have to admit that I didn't *do* anything to make her stop thinking I was a shithead. I grew up by a few weeks and she grew up by a few weeks, and this month, we're having an easier time of it. That's all. I love a rooftop with a view of the city, and even though I bet Don Miguel would shout it all the way across the river if *his* daughter suddenly didn't think *he* was a shithead, I myself am doing my best not to take these things personally.

She loves me.

She loves me not.

Either way, I'm just a human mama-woman doing the best I can.

Five-Foot-Four

It's early yet, but I'm ready to give up the day. Contact lenses out and teeth brushed. Hair down and face washed. The streetlights and the stars can pull their all-nighters.

I've got a Joni Mitchell CD on the player.

"I don't like this," Maia says as she slips off her shoes and ankle socks.

"Put on something else, then. Put on anything you want."

So 2Pac is rapping out of the silver speakers now . . . "God, Mom, stop dancing. You are *so* weird!"

I smile. "If I am weird, you are weird's daughter. You are little baby weird."

And she rolls her eyes. "I'm adopted." She tries to show me the proper dance moves and I try to imitate her. She takes my hands and tries to lead me. Step here, hips this way, step there. I'm concentrating on my bare feet when suddenly she stops cold. "Oh my god!"

I look up. We stand eye to eye. "What?"

She stares at me for a book-length moment, then half-gasps, "I'm as tall as you."

"No way!"

She pulls me into the bathroom to stand back to back in front of the mirror. The mountain of teen beauty products doesn't block our view. I try to creep up onto my tiptoes, but she elbows me. "Feet flat!"

We stand, mama-woman and girl-woman, facing east and west, heads turned slightly toward each other. My memory-camera pans over all the little crayon and Sharpie lines on the white doorframe of her childhood bedroom, the proud markings of her growth through the years. And now here we are: Five-foot-four and five-foot-four. Her rising line meets my own steady measurement. She exhales, excited-worried. "I won't get any taller, will I?"

And I have to admit, "I don't know, honey. You might."

What's Enough

You know as well as I do: I can give you all the advice in the world. I've done boatloads of research to compile what I consider to be the most relevant information available about parenting teens. I've read sixty books and six hundred websites; I've interviewed a hundred parents and four hundred teens.

I am not making this stuff up.

But here's the only thing I can tell you for sure: Whatever is going on, you already have everything you need to meet this moment in your life.

You do not require a makeover.

You have the heart and you have the brain to be the parent your kid needs right now.

Maybe you're not 100% confident. Fifty or 60% will do. Seventy-five is extraordinary. You don't need 100% confidence. What you need is who you are right now—your full strength and energy.

Look at your kid. Or conjure his image in your mind's eye. There he is. You were nervous about feeding him when he was a baby, but you fed him. You were nervous about potty training him when he was a toddler, but you provided him a pot and damned if he can't piss in it. You were nervous when you started schooling him and—*lo and behold*—he learned to read. I thought my kid would never learn to read! I don't even want to tell you what I did to pay for the tutor so I could be sure my kid would learn to read.

Look at your child. If you didn't grow him from microscopic nothing into the person he now is, some woman did. Some human woman.

This child holds your whole heart. Of course you are not 100% confident.

If you feel inadequate, you'll probably do more and give more than is required. This is all right. But it's not necessary. Just as you are, giving just as much as you give, you are enough.

I Wouldn't Wish for Any Other

I asked sixteen- and seventeen-year-olds, "What's great about your parents?"

One of the things that makes my mom a good caregiver is that she tries to learn from her mistakes. One time when she let me go to a party, she didn't give me a curfew. That right there was a mistake. I ended up not coming home until 3:30 or four in the morning. As a result, she didn't let me go anywhere without a reasonable curfew. I love my mom a lot and this just let the love grow fonder.

—Delan, 16

The thing I like most about my parents is their ability to forgive. I know when someone does something to me, I don't want to talk to them at all. When I do something wrong, to have to say sorry takes every ounce of pride I have. But my parents forgive me no matter what.

—Andrew, 16

If you accept your kids for who they want to be, they can find what their interests are. This is one thing my parents have truly gifted me with—the ability to find my own talents in the things I actually love to do. This has left me with a more open opinion than any of my friends for future career possibilities. I consider choosing hobbies like glass blowing, traveling, soccer, MCT (computer stuff), and being a theme park connoisseur.

—Evan, 16

My parents let me make decisions on my own—but we talk about it first. Like drinking, for example. They didn't tell me not to or that I couldn't go to a party because there would be drinking. They just say, "It's your decision." If I got drunk and decided to drive and got in an accident or pulled over by the police, it would be all my fault and no one else's. They say I have to learn on my own, but can get guidance from them when I want it.

—Eric, 17

My parents upset me at times, but I wouldn't wish for any other than them. They're always there for me, and have always helped me to the best of their ability, showing me and teaching me the right path to walk in life. They allow me to make my own decisions and teach me that I must live with the consequences of my actions. Teaching me to help myself, my parents have given me the tools I'll need to survive. I'm so blessed. How many kids these days live with both parents who are married, and have been since before they were born, and still have a promising future for a long-lasting marriage? God bless them. They're really awesome, even though I never tell them.

—Fayanna, 17

For All We Know

*Be open-minded. Just because your child may not be
headed in the exact direction you had planned does not
mean they will not be amazing teenagers and adults.*

—Tisha, 15

As parents, we know a lot of things.

As soon as we decide to let go of sixteen, we can admit that we've
been through it. We've *all* been through it. The leg traps and the heart
wrecks, the drinking problems and the disappointments. We continue
to go through it. We have our experiences. We have a certain amount
of wisdom. We can be fierce about the things that matter to us. We can
let go of the things we don't consider terribly important. We have
some *sense*. We've earned it. We've learned it. As parents, we know a
whole lot of things, and here's one of them: We don't know everything.

When we see our kids heading down a dangerous path, we can
warn them. *Major disappointment there on the left. Raging, bridgeless
river up ahead.* We can do our best to guide them. It is our right and
our responsibility to speak our truths. Sometimes our kids will listen to

us. But as David Bowie has pointed out, sometimes they'll be completely immune to our consultations. We can pray for the best, then, and we can admit this: For all we know, our kids are making the right choices for themselves. For all we know, unexpected perils lurk on the path *we* wanted them to take. For all we know, our kids are a million times more aware of exactly what they're going through than we'll ever be. For all we know, they're following their destinies, learning the things they are meant to learn in precisely the way they are meant to learn them. For all we know, the immense and earthly parental love we have for our children is nothing compared to the devotion their personal god-spirits who watch over them have.

So many fairy tales begin with the death of the too-good mother. Why? Because initiatory adventure is impossible under the constant, watchful eye of a protective parent.

To live as soulful human beings in this world, our kids must develop an inner mother. They can't do that if we remain in complete control of their lives. They can't do that until they allow the too-good mama to—metaphorically—die.

Wise and interesting adults all went through make-or-break crises in their teens or twenties. Maybe a parent warned them about those crises. Maybe not. But those crises ultimately served to embolden them.

Raw, even terrible, experiences make us who we are.

And for all we know, our kids have chosen the exact right moment in their lives to break free from the too-good, protective parent who knows a lot, but doesn't know everything.

Go Ask Inga

Eight P.M. No more work for me tonight. No more classes or meetings for Maia. She's doing her homework in between instant messaging on her laptop.

"Do you want salmon and veggies or tortellini for dinner?" my partner asks her.

Maia opts for the salmon, but now our friend Inga is at the door, grinning. "Did you miss me?"

Maia doesn't move from her position on the couch with her laptop, but these days enthusiasm is relative. "Yes!" she beams without looking up.

It's more passion than she's shown for an adult all week.

I watch Inga. Is she responding to Maia as a human being in a way that I fail to do, or is it just that Inga's not a member of our immediate family?

She invites Maia out for a burrito, and Maia immediately pulls away from the computer, throws a white sweat jacket on over her sporty blue T. She offhandedly denies ever having requested the salmon and vegetables and she's out the door. Burrito time!

Later, Inga will tell me that Maia shunned the burrito in favor of pizza, but what difference does it make? Maia has made a meaningful, if brief, connection with an adult and I'm not going to be the one to complain.

Later, I hope the homework will be done.

Later, I hope the IM will be unplugged.

Later, I hope we'll have a moment before I'm too tired to keep my eyes open as Maia is clicking into her genius hour—ready to select her outfit for tomorrow, ready to plan her entire high school and college careers, ready to contemplate the meaning of life.

"All power to you," I'll say. "But I have to go to bed."

My partner and I eat the salmon and vegetables. A conversation about Korean ecofeminism and why we live in this country morphs into a conversation about how embarrassing it is that we're about to watch the *American Idol* season finale.

Maia and Inga get home just in time for the closing ballads and the much-hyped vote tally. Fox television has us in its greasy palms. The camera pans to the contestants' mothers. One's openly weeping. The other appears to be on Paxil. We want the weeping mama to win. All power to free-flowing emotion.

The whole world might be under siege. The U.S. military is occupying once-sovereign nations. And this is what we're up to: We're cheering for the baby-faced idol on TV, cheering for the weeping mother who's swaying now to the most inane medley rendition of "Let's Get Physical" Olivia Newton-John ever could have nightmared. Almost as many people will cast a ballot in this contest as did in the last presidential election.

Drum roll . . . When the announcement comes, the four of us erupt into cheers from the couch, and then laughter at our own idiocy.

Inga takes her leave, and it's back to the science books for Maia. She's got a few more chemistry problems to solve, and anyway, she has no interest in hanging out with grownups now that the interesting one is gone.

Tomorrow night, Krystee will show up and they'll go to the mall theater to see *Freaky Friday*. Another day, Moe will take her and they'll try to spot celebrities outside an awards show. Fiona will take her to a punk show. Our friend Vanessa will write from California:

I just scored a big new apartment in Santa Cruz.
   Send troubled teens!

                              Love, Vanessa

These are my friends without teenage kids of their own. These are Maia's friends who happen to be grownups. These are the folks who would harbor her if she ever needed a place to stay. The soulful adults in her life who aren't Mom.

As families in America, we are so isolated from one another. And outside families, folks tend to segregate by age. Old and young hardly ever hang out. Americans loved that proverb about its "taking a village" to raise a child, but few had the time or the desire to *be* that village. As parents, then, we often bear sole responsibility for raising our kids. But even if we can be there for our kids twenty-four/seven, our kids lose out when we're the only adults around. What happens when they get bored with us? What happens when they decide we're shitheads? What happens when they need an alternate adult opinion?

What happens when they need a confidant other than a peer?

Maia doesn't usually want to hang out with me at the mall. But she'll get a makeover with Krystee any day.

Kids need soulful grownups in their lives just as they always have—adult friends who aren't entangled in whatever familial dramas we're playing out, who actually enjoy the teen flicks, who aren't blood relations. And the more the merrier.

In Twenty Years

Maia Swift

In twenty years I see myself having graduated high school, and having gotten into one of the best design colleges in the country. I see myself living on the East Coast in a cute cottage house, or maybe more colonial, with my husband and several kids. Names? Chiara (a name I almost got, and that I'm totally in love with!), Melina (the name of a beautiful Italian woman in a forgotten film I once watched)—those are my first choices, and my husband can decide on our sons' names, but I'm thinking like . . . Chris, and Nick.

I want to live in a city where winter is traditional winter: fluffy white snow that lightly falls and makes you feel as though Santa's really coming. Traditional summers: where the grass is still green, and everyone's running through the sprinklers laughing and smiling. Traditional autumn: The only colors in sight are brown, gold, and orange. Leaves are everywhere, and the only thing on people's minds is a grand turkey. Traditional spring: where colors are everywhere—purples, blues, pinks, and yellows, and plants and animals glow.

I'll work for a totally hot clothing store—one that's my favorite now. Maybe Express, or Abercrombie & Fitch. I want to design the clothes—be one of the top designers. I'm going to get paid very well!

I want to still be close with most of my high school friends, and be married to my high school sweetheart.

All of my decisions as a teenager will affect my future in the best of ways—and no regrets. I don't care if my mistakes help me learn and grow. I don't want to make mistakes! I'm making my decisions now.

Adults Will Try to Show You That It Doesn't Exist

A girl in one of my high school writing classes told me, "I used to write novels, but these days I can't find my imagination."

So I asked the whole class of sophomores, "Where does imagination hide?"

> In childhood
> In elementary school
> In your last painted snowman from
>   art class in third grade
> In dreams
> In the back of your mind
> In your cranium
> Inside of you
> In your closet
> In your head
> Soul

It doesn't hide, but adults will try to
    show you that it doesn't exist
In children
On the tip of my tongue
Anywhere it wants to
In the cracks of sadness
In your veins
Way up inside my pencil
In the part of you that's still a kid
In the secrets you will never tell

Spirit

When parents suck and self-esteem is tenuous, when the larger world seems overwhelming and the school scene seems trivial, where does a kid put his trust?

One of the loveliest things about adolescence can be the new and abstract ways in which spirit reveals itself. Younger kids often have complex and endearing spiritual lives—imaginary friends, direct relationships with the miraculous in everyday life, belief in ghosts and angels. With the teen years, we mourn the loss of the child's sense of magical realism. A veil seems to fall between the visible and invisible worlds.

However! Changing winds bring new seeds. Fresh concepts of spirit manifest where old ones become difficult to access.

Where God may have been a white man in the sky—some bony archetype like Santa Claus after Jenny Craig—God may now become a feeling, an overarching presence, a hope.

Where ghosts may have been scary sounds coming from a bedroom closet, ghosts may now become the subtle comfort we feel when whispering truths to loved ones who have passed on.

Where magic may have been perceived everywhere and in every-thing, magic may now become something special, something precious, something sacred.

The childish relationship with spirit, with God, with life, and with death will always glow sweet from the past. But true spiritual journey most often begins in adolescence.

If we are faith-observing folks—or decidedly atheistic—our kids may well question or reject our beliefs. But it's a rare teenager who does no spiritual questing.

Religious recruiters know this. The Gideons stand on public prop-erty just outside Maia's middle school handing out tiny orange Bibles to all the kids. When the "Extreme for Jesus" Nelson Bible company polled teens and learned they weren't reading the Bible because it was "too big and freaky looking," they gave the holy book an "extreme" makeover. The resulting *Revolve,* a bizarre version of the New Testament formatted to look like a fashion magazine, became a national best-seller.

Established religions can be compelling for teenage kids: the sim-plicity of the Taoist Way, the presence and beauty of Hinduism, the clarity of Buddhism and its eightfold path, the earth-based wisdom of paganism, the proactive nature of magic spells, the logic and holiness of Judaism and the inspiration of the kabbalah; the rooting quality of ancestor worship; the passion of Islam; and the love-in-action preached by Jesus. All these traditions provide rules and ideals to live by, the possibility of community and connection, and trust in something bigger than ourselves when life and self feel weak.

As parents, we'll probably want to steer our kids away from what we see as the scarier aspects of some organized religions, but I think it's important to honor the *basis* of our kids' desires to articulate and explore new concepts of spirit and faith.

Even my girl-child recently started asking about going to church. Our family's religious practice had been decidedly unstructured over the years. When my stepdad still gave his radical Catholic Mass on Sundays, we occasionally drove down to attend. When we lived in Oakland, we went to *bembes*—parties for the Orisha spirits. In San Ramon, California, we gathered with other devotees at the feet of the divine mother Ammachi. After we moved to Portland, we visited the Marian Catholic grotto every few months. I myself am an ordained minister of the Universal Life Church. Our house overflows with religious images, ancestor altars, and prayers to the unknown, but we had never been regular churchgoers.

And then the big 1-3. Maia had started getting invited to friends' churches—youth-group sleepovers and the like. She'd been moving toward a renewed faith in God after her atheistic years in elementary school, and now she expressed interest in a traditional Christian community.

"Dear Lord," I thought, "it's time to find us a real church." And so I called around to faith-observing friends and acquaintances. I had in mind something like the left-wing Catholic church I grew up in. I have no beef with Jesus. And I think Mary is a fine lady (she had to deal with a pretty serious teen rebel of her own, that child, arguing with the church elders and whatnot). Still, I needed to avoid the authoritarian bent and fundamentalist flavor of so many Christian churches.

Enter Lani Jo, a dear and reverent friend, who suggested we check out the Episcopal congregation a few miles away. She said the services were similar to Catholic Masses, but the church wasn't under the control of the Vatican. Youth groups, social-justice ministries, ordained women, traditional ceremonies, and liberal theology. They were even about to elect a gay bishop.

"Well, all right."

So off we went, over the freeway and through the rain. To church. Grand red doors and stained-glass panels. Candles lit and prayers whispered. *Church*. That's where you'll find us every Sunday morning—me and my onetime little atheist—singing songs of mercy and exchanging the peace, nibbling white bread and sipping red wine.

What Religion Do I Belong To?

I asked a group of teenagers, "Do you have the same spiritual beliefs as the people who raised you?"

> *My father is a Buddhist, while my mother is a Catholic. When I was a little child, my mother made me go to church every Sunday, and I had to attend church school every week. As I got older, she wasn't as strict and let me quit my church school. My father told me that as long as I have good morals and values and believe in any superior being, it doesn't matter what religion I belong to. I consider myself a Catholic, but some of my beliefs are different than those of most Catholics.*
>
> —Tommy, 17

> *I am Baptist, and so is the rest of my family on my mom's side. I live with her, so naturally we are the same religion. I don't think I could be anything else. I've gone to the same church all of my life.*
>
> —Tramaine, 17

I don't believe in heaven—too clean and perfect. I am a fanatic pessimist. I have a deep-rooted feeling that no one, no matter how saintly, will ever achieve paradise. With this, you need not try for perfection, just be yourself. My parents don't believe this. They still think, after all the "rules" they have broken, that they are going to heaven! I doubt it.

—Ken, 16

The religion I have decided to follow is Wicca mixed with Paganism. This religion teaches that there is a Goddess and a God, and there is some sort of life after death, be it spirithood or reincarnation. I recognize a higher being, the Goddess, who incarnates everything, including the God. My household has no problems with this. Instead of being raised with any particular religion, I was left to my own devices to choose a faith. My mother allows me free reign to dabble in whatever areas I like, to the point of allowing me to go to Sunday school when I was seven to see what they taught. My mother and I participate in theological discussions about different theories and aspects of other religions. Her personal beliefs, which run closely to my own, include acknowledgment of a higher being (for all we know it could be . . . oh, Swiss cheese) and the belief in life—or existence of some sort—after death.

—"Lady Darkmoon," 16

I don't know exactly what I was raised to be, but I grew up going to church every Sunday until the age of ten. I don't go that often now, but I do pray every night before I go to sleep. I suppose my mother has left religion to be my decision to make.

—Trina, 15

225

My grandma was raised in the church and even though my mom doesn't attend church regularly, she sent us with my grandma all the time. I know and understand much of the Bible, and I'm grateful to my grandma for everything she has taught me.

—Mia, 18

I most definitely believe in religious freedom. I am not in any religion; I am neither spiritual nor atheist. I am focused on what is really happening, concrete events in my life and the world around me. I spend time thinking about what I want to do, goals I want to achieve—not praying and listening to the words of an unknown entity. To me, some religions are tools used to control the masses. They may provide healthy morals and values, but ultimately the modern interpretations limit you to a certain path. I have not noticed a uniform benefit to those who believe. If anything, violence and hate increase dramatically as a direct result of religion.

—Devin, 16

Buona Sera, Bella Mamma

Maia has never been the most studious child in the world. She spent the first half of her life on college campuses, but somehow the glory of academics didn't quite seep in. She doesn't lack for intelligence or creativity. It's just that there are so many *other* interesting things to do. The telephone is ringing. She can remember a hundred phone numbers, but not which problems she is supposed to be doing in her math book. The television beckons. She'd rather know what time Shakira will be performing than what year California was admitted to the Union. She's typing away on the IM again. *God, she can type fast.* But she didn't learn it in typing class. She goes to school. She does well. But not because her interest in social studies or algebra comes easily.

Imagine my surprise, then, when Maia announced at the dinner table one summer night that she'd like to enroll in a college-level Italian course downtown.

"Is it for teenagers?" I asked.

"No. It's for everyone."

"Sure. I guess so."

Off she went, then. Girl-child actually volunteering for summer school. Eight weeks. She studied that language book like it was some kind of bible. She insisted on keeping vacations short so as not to interfere with her class schedule. She spent her baby-sitting money on more Italian books and tapes. Goal: fluency.

And when the summer course ended, she asked to sign up for the fall.

She rushes in after class, breathless, rattling off a new phrase or salutation. *"Buona sera, bella Mamma! Come sta?"*

"Sto bene, grazie. E tu?"

"Bene!" And she dashes to her desk to . . . *study*.

I don't know why I'm telling you this story except to say—you never can tell about a person. If interest is organic, a kid might suddenly develop study habits, or anything else they need to reach a goal. It's every unschooler's theory in practice. I didn't do anything special— I didn't do *anything* except say "yes."

She did it.

Comfort Food

And for all their moaning about the hell of home life, I asked fifteen-
and sixteen-year-olds, "What does it taste like, home?"

> Hot chocolate
> Cookies fresh from the oven
> Pink lemonade
> Shepherd's pie
> Brewer's yeast on popcorn
> Strawberry jam
> Apple pie
> Chocolate-chip cookies
> Ice cream
> A fresh breeze
> Beef stew
> Rocks
> Cranberries
> Mac 'n' cheese

Laundry
Mashed potatoes and gravy
Fried rice
Tofu and mushrooms
Chicken soup
Filipino food
Love, hate
Fresh-baked pies
Green chilis
Sushi

Go, Teen, Go!

It's a crazy-beautiful sun-drenched Saturday and I'm sitting on a pale metal bleacher.

The Warriors are scheduled to play their arch rivals, the Quakers, at 1 P.M.

This is the Big Game.

It's Maia's second year on the cheerleading squad, so I've actually *been* to a football game before—something I couldn't say when she first tried out for the team—but I'm hardly in my element. I've picked a spot down in the front row, as far away from the real sports-fan parents as possible. It's not that I dislike them. I'm sure they're pleasant and interesting people, but their raucous shouting hurts my eardrums and makes me feel weirdly anxious and afraid for my life.

The game doesn't actually start at 1 P.M.

Of course it doesn't start at 1 P.M.

The morning game is just barely into its third quarter, I hear someone saying.

The Warriors and the Quakers can't even begin until these other kids clear the field.

The messed-up thing about football is that it doesn't exist on the same time-space continuum as the rest of the universe. I mean, the game is *based* on a clock of sorts, but the referees can and do stop that clock whenever they please. *Time out! Time out! Time out!* They're constantly pausing all action to think about what they've done, or to huddle and discuss.

Imagine if we could just *do* that in real life. *Time out! Time out! Time out!* And not just to meditate for an hour. Everything would actually stop. The clock would freeze. Time's forward motion would cease. All change and chaos and aging would take a break from itself. We could huddle, *discuss.*

At 2 P.M., the crowd starts to thicken. The smell of hot dogs and bubble gum. I guess the other parents and teenage fans have gotten used to the fact that these things don't start on time; that you can pretty much get here whenever you feel like it and the players—all dressed like storm troopers out on the field—will just be getting ready, or milling around, or knocking each other down at whatever yard line.

Half an hour later, and everyone starts yelling all at once, and I'm pretty sure this means the morning game is over. A sunburned dad is giving his tiny football son an aggressive pep talk. "Knock 'em down!" he screams as the boy walks away with his helmet, and then the two new sets of storm troopers file out onto the vast emerald field.

The Warrior cheerleaders, in their green and gold fitted uniforms, take their place on the curved blacktop track. The Quaker girls approach en masse to wish them good luck and then turn, flipping their stringy hair and burgundy skirts. Off to line up at the other side of the track.

The storm troopers are lining up now, too, but nothing gamelike seems to be happening. No matter. Maia and her girls are cheering wild athletic emphatic. Hot as it is, they're "tick, tick, tick, tick, *dy*-na-mite!"

The big electronic sign that's supposed to keep us informed about the game score and the mysterious staccato progress of football time is broken, so I'm even more in need of a clue than usual. But the cheer-leaders seem to have some mystical connection to whatever's going on. Something important has happened on the field now, and sud-denly it's all dancing and singing and boom pow shout. It's all bobbing ponytails and rustling pompoms. It's all held-breath stunts and fly-through-the-air gymnastics. It's all Mom in the bleachers reminding herself that the blacktop track only *looks* like asphalt, that it actually has some padding and some give. It's all free flirtatious fun and chore-ographed hope.

Another cheer mom sits down next to me, clutching a bag of fries. "Is it half time yet?" she wants to know.

"Beats me."

Someone makes a touchdown and I'm not quite sure who it is, but the whole squad starts to cheer, smiling as they threaten to stomp the other team and promising a long and spirited fight. The girls turn back to the field, resting at attention, hands behind their backs.

The cheer mom next to me sucks on a fry. "My eldest just moved out," she says, then gestures to the cheering girls. "Have you realized these kids only have four more summers at home—if we're lucky?"

I nod.

Lucky.

Four summers.

Fourteen summers already gone.

It hardly seems possible now that Maia's infantile cries so

unnerved me, that her toddler tantrums made me pull my hair out. "Trichotillomania," my therapist called it. How often did I pause to appreciate the irrational love, dahlias in the kitchen sink, the smooth wooden toys? It hardly seems possible that I was so desperate for my girl-child to learn to walk and talk, to read and write; that the quaint dramas of elementary school made me long for this coming maturity. Even these days, I find myself looking forward and through. *We just have to survive this stage,* I think. Like on camping trips when I'm so busy swatting mosquitoes, I hardly notice the effervescent beauty of the Sierras. *Time out! Time out! Time out!* I want to yell. I just need a little time to huddle, *discuss.*

It's coming on 4 P.M. and I'm about to pass out from heat exhaustion. I'm mildly disturbed by the viciousness of competition, but there's also something pure and luminous about this whole scene. Pompoms in the air. A world where time can start and stop without apparent logic. A world where I never, *ever,* have to worry about giving advice. A world where I can freely admit that I have no idea what's going on.

I just sit in the pale metal bleachers, beaming, content. Because Maia is the teenager now. And this is *her* world. The clock is on. The clock is off. The clock is on again. We can't know because the sign is broken, but we can still cheer for the best outcome.

A flush magnificence, and suddenly everybody's yelling crazy beautiful from the stands, and I'm sure this means someone has won, and thank god because it's practically sunset, and, no, this isn't any way I ever dreamed I would spend a day, but here I am.

Bibliography

The American Heritage Dictionary of the English Language. Fourth Edition. New York: Houghton Mifflin Company, 2000.

Anorexia Nervosa and Related Eating Disorders, Inc. www.anred.com. (September 2003)

Army Junior ROTC. www.armyrotc.com/spec.html. (May 2003)

Bright, Kimberly. "A Close Encounter with Nina Hagen." *Hip Mama* 28, Spring, 2003.

Brownless, Shannon. "Inside the Teen Brain." *U.S. News & World Report,* August 9, 1999.

Chödrön, Pema. *The Places That Scare You: A Guide to Fearlessness in Difficult Times.* Boston: Shambhala Classics, 2001.

Davis-Thompson, Esther. *Raising Up Queens: Loving Our Daughters Loud and Strong.* Philadelphia: Innisfree Press, 2000.

Erikson, Erik H. *Identity and the Life Cycle.* New York: W.W. Norton & Co., 1994.

Essential Astrology. www.essentialastrology.co.uk. (August 2003)

GirlMom community. www.girlmom.com. (May, June, and September 2003)

Gleick, James. *Chaos: The Making of a New Science.* New York: Penguin Books, 1987.

Good News Network. "US Teens Get Along with Parents." September 8, 2003.

Greydanus, Donald, and Philip Bashe. *Caring for Your Teenager: The Complete and Authoritative Guide.* New York: Bantam Books, 2003.

Grudin, Robert. *Time and the Art of Living.* New York: Ticknor and Fields, 1982.

Harris, Gardiner. "Suicide alert revives qualms on antidepressants." *International Herald Tribune,* August 8, 2003.

Howe, Neil, and William Strauss. *Millennials Rising: The Next Great Generation.* New York: Vintage, 2000.

Lao-tzu. *Tao Te Ching.* Translated by Ursula K. Le Guin. Boston: Shambhala Books, 1997.

Llewellyn, Grace. *The Teenage Liberation Handbook: How to Quit School and Get a Real Life and Education.* Eugene, Ore.: Lowry House, 1991.

McBride, Angela Barron, Ph.D. *The Secret of a Good Life With Your Teenager.* New York: Times Books, 1987.

The Media Project. www.themediaproject.com. (April and October 2003)

Millennial Manifesto. Available at www.millennialpolitics.com. (August 2003)

Muffy Magazine, "Adolescence" issue (fall/winter 2002).

Quart, Alissa. *Branded: The Buying and Selling of Teenagers.* New York: Perseus Publishing, 2003.

Religious Tolerance. www.religioustolerance.org. (September 2003)

Riera, Michael, Ph.D. *Uncommon Sense for Parents with Teenagers.* Berkeley: Celestial Arts, 1995.

Ruiz, Don Miguel. *The Four Agreements: A Toltec Wisdom Book.* San Rafael, Calif.: Amber-Allen Publishing, 1997.

Serazio, Michael. "An Rx for Trouble?" Columbia News Service, April 4, 2003.

Slater, Lauren. "Repress Yourself." *New York Times,* February 23, 2003.

Teal, Celeste. *Identifying Planetary Triggers: Astrological Techniques for Prediction.* St. Paul, Minn.: Llewellyn Publications, 2000.

Wilhelm, Richard, and Cary F. Baynes, translators, *The I Ching* or *Book of Changes.* Princeton: Princeton University Press, 1972.

Wolf, Anthony E., Ph.D. *Get Out of My Life, But First Could You Drive Me and Cheryl to the Mall?* Revised and updated edition. New York: Farrar Straus Giroux, 2002.

Wolcott, James. "Teen Engine: Riding with the Kid Culture," *Vanity Fair,* July 2003.

Young, Cathy. "The Virtue of Stoicism." *Boston Globe,* March 3, 2003.

Resources and Emergency Hotlines
Hook It Up

Don't try and do it alone. Link up to a community.
Being a hero is basically arrogance.

—Mama Lynn

Mercifully, when it comes to parenting teens, there are countless cool resources on the Internet and in our communities. The trick is to find them. Here are a few emergency numbers, media resources, and organizations that can help us hook up with the helpful folks. Look for more at www.whatevermom.com. And have a lovely, unboring day.

Alcohol- and Drug-Abuse Hotlines

National Council on Alcoholism and Drug Dependence (NCADD)

Their Hope Line will refer callers to a local affiliate office. Callers can also leave their name and address to receive written information about alcohol and other drug abuse.

(800) NCA-CALL / (800) 622-2255

National Drug and Alcohol Treatment Referral Service

The Center for Substance Abuse Treatment provides information; local treatment options; and advice on alcohol, drug, and family problems.

(800) 662-HELP / (800) 662-4357

Alternative Media

Beauty Magazine

An online magazine out of Canada that "challenges the ways in which we think about real beauty—how the media affects us, personal stories, body image, dieting, eating disorders—all the things that constitute the opinion we have of ourselves."

www.beautymagazine.ca

The Coalition for Positive Sexuality

Asserting teens' right to complete and honest sex education, this popular website offers information, resources, and a teen forum on sex and sexuality because "sex is enjoyable when everyone involved is into it, and when everyone has the information they need to take care of themselves and each other."

www.positive.org

Hip Mama

My zine for progressive parents!
Subscriptions available for $15 online at www.hipmamashop.com, or
via good, old-fashioned mail order.
www.hipmama.com
P.O. Box 12525
Portland, OR 97212

Sex, Etc.

A sex-ed website and newsletter by and for teens. They write, "We,
the teen writers and editors of Sex, Etc., believe that all teens deserve
honest, medically-accurate and balanced information about human
sexuality—so that we can make responsible choices about our sexual
health." Free subscriptions available online.
www.sxetc.org

Teen Voices

"Because you're more than just a pretty face." An online and print
magazine written by, for, and about teen girls and young women.
Articles cover issues from racial identity to body image, spirituality to
activism. For a subscription to the print magazine (four issues), send a
check for $19.95 to Women Express, Inc.
www.teenvoices.com
Women Express, Inc.
P.O. Box 120–027
Boston, MA 02112-0027
(888) 882-TEEN / (888) 882-8336

Youth Outlook (YO!)

An online and print magazine by and about young adults. To subscribe to the print magazine, send a check for $25 made out to Pacific News Service, or subscribe online for $15.

www.youthoutlook.org
275 Ninth Street
San Francisco, CA 94103
(415) 503-4170

WireTap

"Youth in pursuit of the dirty truth." A project of AlterNet and the Independent Media Institute, WireTap is an independent information source for socially conscious and activist youth.

www.wiretapmag.org
E-mail: info@wiretapmag.org

Civil Rights Organizations

The American Civil Liberties Union (ACLU)

The ACLU fights civil liberties violations. Most of their clients are ordinary people who have experienced an injustice and decided to fight back. Contact information for regional offices is available on the website.

www.aclu.org
125 Broad Street, 18th Floor
New York, NY 10004

U.S. Commission on Civil Rights

The U.S. Commission on Civil Rights collects information relating to discrimination or a denial of equal protection of the law because of race, color, religion, sex, age, disability, or national origin, and serves as a clearinghouse for information about discrimination.

www.usccr.gov
624 Ninth Street NW
Washington, DC 20425
(202) 376-7533

National Gay and Lesbian Task Force (NGLTF)

A national progressive organization working for the civil rights of gay, lesbian, bisexual, and transgender people.

www.ngltf.org
1325 Massachusetts Avenue NW, Suite 600
Washington, DC 20005
(202) 393-5177
E-mail: ngltf@ngltf.org

The National Organization for Women (NOW)

The largest organization of feminist activists in the United States.

www.now.org
733 15th Street NW, 2nd Floor
Washington, DC 20005
(202) 628-8669

Parents, Families and Friends of Lesbians and Gays (PFLAG)

Information, support, and advocacy for gays, lesbians, bisexuals, and transgendered people and their families.

www.pflag.org
1726 M Street NW, Suite 400
Washington, DC 20036
(202) 467-8180

Office of Civil Rights
The Office of Civil Rights—which is, weirdly, part of the U.S. Department of Agriculture—deals with discrimination cases in federally funded educational institutions. You can ask for information or get a regional number where you can file a complaint.
www.usda.gov/cr
USDA Office of Civil Rights
1400 Independence Avenue SW, Mail Stop 9410
Washington, DC 20250
(202) 720-5964

Conscientious Objectors to Militarization

Central Committee for Conscientious Objectors (CCCO)
Provides resources, information, a newsletter, books, and videos presenting alternative perspectives on war and militarization. The CCCO can also provide referrals to local speakers who can come to your kid's school or speak to kids about alternatives to the military.
www.objector.org
630 20th Street
Oakland, CA 94612
(510) 465-1617
(215) 563-8787
E-mail: info@objector.org

Women Against Military Madness
Hundreds of women and men empowered to make social change through volunteer activism.
www.worldwidewamm.org
310 E. 38th Street, #222
Minneapolis, MN 55409
(612) 827-5364

Food, Nutrition, and Eating-Disorder Help

National Association of Anorexia Nervosa and Associated Disorders (ANAD)
Provides information about eating disorders and referrals to treatment.
www.anad.org
(847) 831-3438

Bulimia and Self-Help Hotline
Twenty-four-hour crisis line.
(314) 588-1683

Fueling the Teen Machine
Fueling the Teen Machine, by dietitians Ellen Shanley and Colleen Thompson, presents the latest information on everything from carbohydrates and vitamins to eating disorders and vegetarianism. Bull Publishing, 2001.

Food Stamp Program
Visit the government's Food Stamp Program website to find your state's Food Stamp hotline number.
www.fns.usda.gov/fsp/contact_info/hotlines.htm

Eating Disorder Referral and Information Center
International treatment referrals and prevention information.
www.edreferral.com
(858) 792-7463
E-mail: edreferral@aol.com

Real Gorgeous: The Truth About Body and Beauty
Kaz Cooke's *Real Gorgeous* is a funny, reassuring read about fashion fibs and diet myths for teens and young women. W.W. Norton & Company, 1996.

Something Fishy
A website full of information and resources on eating disorders and fighting the body police.
www.something-fishy.org

VegWeb
Online information, resources, chats, and recipes for vegans and vegetarians.
http://vegweb.com/

Health Care

American Holistic Health Association (AHHA)
Resources and referrals to holistic-health practitioners, with a searchable online database.
www.ahha.org
P.O. Box 17400
Anaheim, CA 92817-7400
(714) 779-6152
E-mail: mail@ahha.org

Cancer Information Service
A free public service of the National Cancer Institute.
http://cis.nci.nih.gov/
(800) 4-CANCER / (800) 422–6237

Teens T.A.P. (Teens Teaching AIDS Prevention)
The only national hotline founded by teens for teens. It provides education and information about how to prevent the transmission of HIV. Teens staff the toll-free hotline weekdays 4:00 P.M. to 8:00 P.M. (Central Time).
(800) 234-TEEN / (800) 234-8336

National AIDS Hotline
This twenty-four-hour hotline is run by the Centers for Disease Control and Prevention.
(800) 342-AIDS / (800) 342-2437

National Certification Commission for Acupuncture and Oriental Medicine
Provides information and referrals to local certified acupuncturists and Oriental-medicine practitioners. See their website for a searchable database.
www.nccaom.org
11 Canal Center Plaza, Suite 300
Alexandria, VA 22314
E-mail: info@nccaom.org

Homeschooling / Unschooling

Not Back to School Camp
Coordinated by teen-liberation guru Grace Llewellyn, this camp for teenage unschoolers is in its tenth year. About a hundred kids show up for each week-long session in August and September. Held outside Eugene, Oregon, the camp costs about five hundred dollars for the week. Scholarships available.
www.nbtsc.org
P.O. Box 1014
Eugene, OR 97440
(541) 686-2315
E-mail: NBTSC@aol.com

Jon's Homeschool Resources
Probably the oldest, most comprehensive collection of homeschooling links on the Internet.
www.midnightbeach.com/hs

The Teenage Liberation Handbook

First published over a decade ago, Grace Llewellyn's classic unschooling manual *The Teenage Liberation Handbook: How to Quit School and Get a Real Life and Education* has been revised and updated. "Your life, time, and brain should belong to you, not an institution. This handbook is for everyone who has ever gone to school, but it is especially a book for teenagers and people with teenagers in their lives." Lowry House Publishers, 1998.
www.lowryhousepublishers.com

School-Free

An online info source by and for teenage unschoolers containing articles and resources. Teens answer questions about the unschooler's life.
http://info.nbtsc.org/schoolfree/

Therapy Referrals

1-800 THERAPIST Network

International mental-health referral service.
(800) THERAPIST / (800) 843-7274

Find-a-Therapist

International online database of mental-health professionals, including psychiatrists, psychologists, social workers, marriage and family therapists, and pastoral counselors.
http://find-a-therapist.com/

Runaways and Missing Children

You do *not* have to wait twenty-four hours to file a missing-persons report with the police. Call 911.

Greyhound "Home Free" Program

Greyhound Lines will provide free one-way transportation between any two points in the continental United States (excluding Alaska) for runaway kids returning home. To receive a free ride, children between the ages of twelve and eighteen should call the National Runaway Switchboard at (800) 621-4000.

www.greyhound.com

National Center for Missing and Exploited Children (NCMEC)

A clearinghouse of information about missing and exploited children, NCMEC provides assistance to individuals and law-enforcement agencies in the prevention and investigation of cases involving missing and exploited children, and distributes photographs and descriptions of missing children worldwide. Call 911, then call these guys.

www.missingkids.org

Charles B. Wang International Children's Building

699 Prince Street

Alexandria, VA 22314-3175

(800) THE-LOST / (800) 843-5678

National Runaway Switchboard

A free and confidential twenty-four-hour hotline offering counseling, advice, and emergency-service help for teens, parents, and friends. For teens: "Are you thinking about running away? Have you already run away and need to find a place to stay, food, clothing, legal or medical

assistance?" For parents: "Are you afraid your child might be thinking about running away? Do you know what to do when she does? Will you know what to do when he returns home after running away?"
www.nrscrisisline.org
3080 N. Lincoln Ave.
Chicago, IL 60657
(800) 621-4000

Suicide Prevention

National Adolescent Suicide Hotline
A twenty-four-hour crisis line answered by the National Runaway Switchboard.
(800) 621-4000

National Suicide Hotline
Trained volunteers and professional counselors there to listen.
(888) SUICIDE / (800) 784-2433
For an online list of local and national suicide hotlines, see www.suicidehotlines.com.

Teen Pregnancy and Parenting

Girls Inc.
"A national nonprofit youth organization dedicated to inspiring all girls to be strong, smart and bold," Girls Inc. offers numerous programs for teen girls, including teen-pregnancy prevention and support to teen moms.

www.girlsinc.org
120 Wall Street
New York, NY 10005-3902
(800) 374-4475

girlMom
One kick-ass online community for the support and empowerment of teen parents.
www.girlmom.com

Planned Parenthood
Birth control, Pap smears, abortion services, and referrals for other women's health-care needs. To schedule an appointment at your nearest location, call (800) 230-PLAN / (800) 230-7526.
www.plannedparenthood.org
E-mail: communications@ppfa.org

Antiviolence and Self-Defense Info

Assistance for Gay and Lesbian Victims of Hate Crimes
Help and information even for those who choose not to call the police.
(915) 562-GAYS / (915) 562-4297
www.lambda.org/

Home Alive
A Seattle-based antiviolence project offering affordable self-defense classes and public education. Website lists national as well as local resources.

www.homealive.org
(206) 720-0606
E-mail: selfdef@homealive.org

National Domestic-Violence Hotlines
Crisis intervention, referrals, information, and support for the victims of domestic violence and their families and friends.
National Domestic Violence Hotline: (800) 799-SAFE / (800) 799-7233
National Child Abuse Hotline: (800) 422-4453

National Hate Crime Reporting Hotline
This is a Justice Department office where you can report hate crimes.
(800) 347-HATE / (800) 347-4283

Rape, Abuse & Incest National Network (RAINN)
A twenty-four-hour hotline for survivors of sexual assault who can't reach a rape crisis center through a local telephone call, as well as for those who might not know that a local center exists.
(800) 656-HOPE / (800) 656-4673

Self-Injury Help by S.A.F.E. (Self-Abuse Finally Ends)
Provides treatment for adolescents and adults who engage in deliberate, repeated self-injurious behavior. Free written information on self-injury is available.
(800) DONT-CUT / (800) 366-8288

Sexual Assault Crisis Line
National twenty-four-hour hotline providing support and local referrals.
(800) 643-6250

VOICES in Action
International organization providing assistance to survivors of incest
and child sexual abuse—if you need help or someone to talk to.
(800) 7-VOICE-8 / (800) 786-4238

Acknowledgments

Major thanks to the hundreds of teens, parents, and others who were so generous with their thoughts and writings for this book. Especially to China Martens, editor-publisher of the zine *The Future Generation*, who shared her reflections on parenting an older teen, then lent her genius mind and great big brave heart to the editing process. Thanks to Oregon Literary Arts/Writers in the Schools and all my amazing students at Grant, Cleveland, and Benson high schools. Thanks to Leslie Miller and everyone at Seal Press for cheerleading me through the writing and editing. Thanks to Inga Aaron for her valuable insights, to Inga Muscio for the research ideas and self-esteem shots, to Gabrielle for her library research, to Krystee Sidwell for her most excellent feedback on the drafted manuscript, to Maria Fabulosa for making me coffee and feeding me while I wrote, and for more editing. And, of course, major cosmic thanks to Maia, who always met her deadlines and never let me change a word.

About the Author

Ariel Gore is Maia's mom and editor-publisher of *Hip Mama,* the award-winning zine covering the culture and politics of motherhood. She's authored two other parenting books, *The Hip Mama Survival Guide* and *The Mother Trip;* a memoir, *Atlas of the Human Heart;* and co-edited *Breeder.* You can write her at P.O. Box 12525, Portland, OR 97212, or go to www.whatevermom.com.

Selected Titles from Seal Press

The Mother Trip: Hip Mama's Guide to Staying Sane in the Chaos of Motherhood by Ariel Gore. $14.95, 1-58005-029-8. In a book that is part self-help, part critique of the mommy myth, and part hip-mama handbook, Ariel Gore offers support to mothers who break the mold.

Breeder: Real-Life Stories from the New Generation of Mothers edited by Ariel Gore and Bee Lavender, foreword by Dan Savage. $16.00, 1-58005-051-4. From the editors of *Hip Mama*, this hilarious and heartrending compilation creates a space where Gen-X moms can dish, cry, scream, and laugh.

Mother Shock: Loving Every (Other) Minute of It by Andrea J. Buchanan. $14.95, 1-58005-082-4. One new mom's refreshing and down-to-earth look at the birth of a mother.

Toddler: Real-life Stories of Those Fickle, Irrational, Urgent, Tiny People We Love edited by Jennifer Margulis. $14.95, 1-58005-093-X. These clever, succinct, and poignant tales capture all the hilarity, magic, and chaos of raising the complex little people we call toddlers.

The Big Rumpus: A Mother's Tale from the Trenches by Ayun Halliday. $15.95, 1-58005-071-9. Creator of the wildly popular *East Village Inky*, Halliday describes the quirks and everyday travails of a young urban family, warts and all.

Growing Seasons: Half-baked Garden Tips, Cheap Advice on Marriage and Questionable Theories on Motherhood by Annie Spiegelman. $14.95, 1-58005-079-4. A celebration of family in all its comfort and complexity.

Seal Press publishes many books of fiction and nonfiction by women writers. Please visit our Web site at **www.sealpress.com.**